Richard Briggs has been Lecturer in New Testament and Hermeneutics at All Nations Christian College in Hertfordshire since 1999, and before that was involved in church ministry in London and in Nottingham. A published author, his previous books include *Words in Action* (T&T Clark, 2001), *It's Been a Quiet Week in the Global Village* (SPCK/Triangle, 1999) and a collection of short stories about the joys and setbacks of mission work, based on his own experiences around the world. He is married and has three children.

READING THE BIBLE WISELY

Richard Briggs

Baker Academic
A Division of Baker Book House Co
Grand Rapids, Michigan 49516

© 2003 by Richard Briggs

Published by Baker Academic
a division of Baker Book House Company
P.O. Box 6287, Grand Rapids, MI 49516-6287
www.bakeracademic.com

Printed in the United Kingdom

Library of Congress Cataloging-in-Publication Data is on file
at the Library of Congress, Washington, D.C.

ISBN 0-8010-2654-7

Contents

To Joshua
who has helped me to see many things,
including the Bible,
with open eyes

Introduction

What does it mean to read the Bible wisely? This book tackles some familiar concerns about how to interpret the Bible and how to think about the Bible, with the goal of answering that question.

Bible readers often, in my view, become worried by the wrong question: how can we know that our interpretation is right, and that this text can't mean something else? Perhaps it can mean pretty much anything. If you set your mind to it, you can do just about anything with the biblical text. We all know the funny stories about verses taken out of context. Take my friend Paul, for example, who was wondering whether to continue in Christian work in Madrid or move on, and who opened up his Bible one day to Acts 19 and read about Paul in the city of Ephesus, that he 'stayed in the city for 2 more years', speaking boldly about the Kingdom of God. That made his decision for him. Is there anything wrong with that? Does it all depend on what we are looking for?

One student at the college where I work was answering a question which required them to comment on points of interest in the opening chapters of Job, and came to Job 2.9 which contains the startling report that 'his wife said to him, "Do you still persist in your integrity? Curse God and die."' There is quite a lot worth commenting on in that verse, from all sorts of angles. They wrote: 'from this verse we can tell that Job had a wife'.

Whether the biblical text *can* mean whatever we want is

1

not the point. What it *can* mean often tells us more about ourselves than about the text. What it *does in practice* mean is really the issue. What makes for an appropriate way to read the Bible? Put differently: what is the goal of Bible reading? Why read the Bible?

My observation is that most people read the Bible for one or both of two reasons: it will tell them about God, and it will help them understand how to live. This is a fair way to start out reading the Bible. But our experience rapidly suggests that things are more complex than this, and two further questions soon arise: how *should* we read the Bible, and what should we think *about* the Bible? At this point a variety of things can happen, as we begin to think more reflectively about Bible reading. This book is designed to help that process.

In this book I assume a reader who is interested in reading the Bible, has perhaps read quite a lot of it, heard it preached frequently, and would agree that Bible reading is good for knowing God and knowing how to live. But the reader is also aware that the Bible is interpreted in a variety of ways, many of them mutually contradictory. Arguments about the Bible, about its nature and about how to interpret it, are among the most bitter and divisive that Christians generally experience, right after arguments about worship styles and service times. And the barest familiarity with the Bible demonstrates beyond doubt that it is not at all the sort of 'handbook for living' that we might have expected. So what are we to do?

Typically we do two things at the same time, especially if we are beginning to study the Bible seriously, and these two things do not usually sit well together. First we learn about 'hermeneutics'. Hermeneutics is the art (or science) of inter-pretation, and if we are talking about the Bible then it is both biblical interpretation and it is also the process of thinking about and evaluating biblical interpretation. The first part of this book is about hermeneutics, but rather than talk hermeneutical theory I have tried to introduce the theory by focusing on particular biblical passages and showing what sorts of questions about interpretation they raise. Hermeneutical thinking, I am convinced, is an essential part of the skills and tools necessary for good Bible reading.

The second thing we do is we start to construct theories about what sort of book the Bible is. This is less a hermeneutical task than a theological one: it is the construction of what is normally called a 'doctrine of Scripture'. This is also an important task. The problem is that it is often done in relative isolation from the first, hermeneutical, task. We start to talk about the Bible as, in some sense, the Word of God, or at the very least as the book which God wants us to read. If we are not careful, we will find ourselves handling the Bible in almost a 'pre-hermeneutical' way as we pick out verses which prove this or that view of biblical authority or inspiration, or whatever our chosen topic is. In the second part of the book I start to focus on these 'doctrinal' questions, but again I try to let a study of various biblical passages show how the doctrines arise from the nature of the biblical text that we study.

The linking of these two different approaches is a complicated matter, and it is not helped by the fact that academic specialization tends to mean that those who write books on hermeneutics are often not talking about the doctrine of Scripture, and vice versa. On a simple introductory level, it is still common to find introductions to biblical interpretation which talk about how to interpret lots of different styles of biblical writing, or look at how to find out what an author wanted to say, but which do not address theologically the question of what difference it makes that the book we are looking at is the Bible. In theory it could be true that the Bible could be interpreted like any other book, and in some areas this manifestly is true (how to work out the meanings of words, how to understand sentence construction, and so forth), but it seems more likely that the uniqueness of the Bible requires some ways of interpreting it that are also unique.

More to the point, we need ways of thinking about the Bible which explicitly hold together the hermeneutical and the doctrinal approaches. What is the poor Bible reader, let alone pastor or preacher, to make of this split between 'biblical studies' and 'theology'? The former will teach us that 1 Corinthians is part of Paul's correspondence in the mid-50s with a church in Corinth and that we have to read it 'contextually', while the latter will direct us to particular verses in it and deduce all sorts of theological propositions, ranging from whether women are to be silent in church to views on idolatry, homosexuality and the resurrection. Hermeneutics, it seems to me, is the discipline which offers us a way ahead here, and this book is intended as an exercise in leading the reader into the specific issues which arise when reading the Bible, not out of the sheer ingenuity of the reader looking for something novel to talk about, but out of the text itself, and in particular out of the details and the specifics of the text as they relate to the big (theological) picture.

Hermeneutics is a notoriously jargon-laden area. I have endeavoured to avoid all the jargon as much as I can, and when I have needed a technical term I have tried both to show why it is needed and define it clearly. I also appeal to the details of the text a lot and, since I end up mainly talking about the New Testament, this sometimes means talking about details of the Greek text. But the aim of doing this is simply to show why a certain issue is raised in a certain way, and no knowledge of Greek is assumed. That it is the New Testament which is mainly in view was not for any profound or theological reason: I just happen to be more familiar with seeing

4

how hermeneutical issues arise out of it than with the Old Testament, but in principle much of what follows could be re-expressed to show how it works with the Old Testament too. I have in general chosen the road less footnoted, since there seem to be enough footnotes in the world already, but it is only right to say where specific points have come from, and at the end I try to acknowledge my debts.

Part One of the book, then, explores hermeneutical issues to do with reading the Bible in an appropriate context. What kind of context could that be?

It could be a historical context: Jesus' ministry on earth occupied a certain historical period and many of its details will remain obscure to us if we are not willing to invest in understanding the era on its own terms. Some would go further: not just the details but even the whole reason behind Jesus' ministry must remain obscure to us if we do not grasp this time period in all its particular detail.

It could be a literary context. What sort of writing is a gospel? Is it like a biography or a modern history book or a work of theology? How do we interpret stories Jesus told or accounts of acts that he performed?

It could be a theological context. What makes a written account of Jesus different from, say, a written account of a Roman emperor of the time? We talk of miracles in the Gospel accounts: what makes them different from any other mighty acts performed at the time of Jesus? What makes Jesus' parables theologically different from the other parables told at the time? Why, fundamentally, does the New Testament carry that title: 'new' in what sense? What does 'testament' mean? We can say straight away that it means 'covenant', but what does it mean to say that the New Testament is a 'new covenant'?

The understanding of these three different types of context, which inevitably overlap in some ways, occupies Part One, as well as recurring in various places later on. The Gospel of Luke turns out to provide us with clear examples for all these three cases.

In Part Two, we turn to consider specific doctrines about the Bible: its clarity, its inspiration, and its authority, and ask what it means in practice to read the Bible as an inspired text or as an authoritative text. Again, I attempt to show how these doctrines relate to the reading of actual Bible passages.

Throughout, my conviction is that what we are looking for is an approach to the Bible which captures the essence of *wisdom*: a way to read the Bible wisely. Wisdom is not a heavily valued idea in our modern and/or postmodern world. We value choice, originality, interest, sincerity, therapy, even profit and success, and the Christian world is sadly full of books mirroring just these values: quick-fix 'how to' books on church, prayer, relationships, and indeed on how to read the Bible.

Bible reading is a spiritual discipline, both like and unlike any other. Like any spiritual discipline it requires maturity and wisdom, as well as a reading context of other Christians to support and challenge us. At the same time it is not like any other discipline, since it has its own technical requirements with which most of us are not so familiar. I have been surprised but delighted to discover that the book of Revelation offers a powerful example of how to bring these two lines of thinking together, and thus the final chapter of the book turns its eyes heavenwards, whichever way that turns out to be, to attempt to integrate the various insights. That Revelation should occupy the seventh of the seven chapters was, it must be said, simply too good an opportunity to miss.

As this final chapter suggests, and as the emphasis on wisdom indicates too, our goal throughout is to learn to read the Bible with open eyes, but the gift of eyes to see is a gift that only God can give, a point that I draw out in a concluding reflection. But if we are in any sense reading the Bible in order to know God, then perhaps that is precisely the way it should be.

♦ Part One ♦

INTERPRETING
THE BIBLICAL TEXT

♦

◆ 1 ◆

Reading the Bible as Christian Scripture: The Road to Emmaus

Luke 24.13–35

◆

The Emmaus story is something of a classic for allowing us to focus on issues of biblical interpretation. The reasons will become clear as we follow the two disciples along the road. The journey takes us out from Jerusalem in something of a north-westerly direction towards Emmaus, although the 'sixty stadia' given as the distance, roughly seven miles, appears to put us some considerable way beyond the probable site of Emmaus, an early indication that the road to biblical interpretation is rarely straightforward.

The passage starts 'on the same day': the day that the women and the apostles have arrived at the empty tomb, puzzled and amazed. Two of them are walking along, one of whom is named in v. 18 as Cleopas. The other is unnamed, perhaps Luke himself, modestly hiding his identity rather as John does in the Fourth Gospel, or perhaps Cleopas's wife, and thus a couple about to have their eyes opened rather as the first couple, Adam and Eve, did, only with a very different result. Perhaps we just do not know who Cleopas's companion is, which seems to me most likely, and a gentle reminder that the pursuit of detail is not always fruitful.

They are joined on the road by a third companion, 'but their eyes were kept from recognizing him' (v. 16). This surely does not mean that they could not spot the likeness, as if they were

11

haunted by a vague feeling that they had seen him somewhere before, but just could not quite remember where. Luke does not elaborate, or say who it is who keeps them from recognition, but perhaps the text invites us to assume that this is God's work, for reasons which are obviously still veiled in obscurity at this point, since our eyes have not yet become accustomed to picking out the details of this kind of story.

Jesus leads them into a discussion of 'the things' which have occurred recently, managing to get Cleopas to say to him, of all people, that he is the only stranger who does not know what has happened in these last few days in Jerusalem. What is the point here? If nothing else, Cleopas demonstrates that the knowledge of the death and crucifixion of Jesus is very much public knowledge. More than this: in vv. 22–4 he reports the astonishing turn of events by which they have all come to see that the tomb is empty, the body is gone, and now the only thing which is sure is that *nobody really knows what is going on*. Cleopas does not use these exact words, or at least Luke polishes them up if he did, but the point is established as clearly as we could wish, and it turns out to be an important point. The facts are all in, as it were, and they do not add up. The tomb is empty, the angels have been seen (by women, which may be why Cleopas is particularly unsure what to make of it, since women's testimony on its own was a much debated issue at the time), there were all these hopes riding on Jesus, and now nobody knows what to make of it. It is good to read slowly enough to pick up all these details. Sometimes we read these stories so fast, and with a kind of vague familiarity, that we can miss the way that the story develops and aims to surprise us.

The broad outline is perhaps very familiar. Jesus responds to Cleopas, explaining that, on the contrary, all is not lost, but that 'it was necessary that the Messiah should suffer these things and then enter into his glory' (v. 26). He interprets

12

Moses and all the prophets for them, they walk on to the village, he stays and breaks bread with them, and in v. 31 their eyes are opened, and they recognize him. He vanishes, but they, inspired and now fully energized, return to the apostles and proclaim that 'the Lord has risen indeed!' Now it all makes sense. Now they have not just the facts, but a picture which puts the facts in context and which adds up. It adds up, let us note, in ways which they had not anticipated. Luke first showed us a scene of information with confusion: the necessary prelude to understanding and insight. By the end of the story, the two who set out on the road from Jerusalem are back where they started, but their world has changed. The journey along the road to Emmaus, as captured in this story, invites us to a similar sort of journey in our own understanding: a pilgrimage into insight and wisdom. It is worth picking out in more detail some of the ways in which Luke 24 leads us into our own journey of biblical interpretation.

In his commentary on Luke's Gospel, Joel Green suggests the following structure for the Emmaus story:

> The Journey from Jerusalem (vv. 14–15)
>   Appearance, 'Obstructed Eyes', Lack of Recognition (16)
>   Interaction (17–18)
>   Summary of 'the things' (19–21)
>   Empty Tomb and Vision (22–3a)
>   *Jesus is Alive* (23b)
>   Empty Tomb, but No Vision (24)
>   Interpretation of 'the things' (25–7)
>   Interaction (28–30)
>   'Opened Eyes', Recognition, and Disappearance (31–2)
> The Journey to Jerusalem (33–5)[1]

It is set out in this way to highlight the 'there-and-back' structure of the story. It starts and ends in Jerusalem, it includes eyes being obstructed and opened, it includes two 'interactions' or dialogues on the road, and 'the things' which happened in Jerusalem are both summarized and interpreted. At the centre of the story, on this view, is the declaration that Jesus is alive (v. 23). This kind of structure of a biblical story is known as a *chiasm*, so-called after the shape of the Greek letter χ (*chi*), which looks like our 'X'. It is a way of showing that a story has a symmetric structure in itself.

Why would we notice this? It is important to realize at this point that the layout of the original Greek copy of the Gospel of Luke, as of any New Testament manuscript, would be one continuous written text: one letter after another with no breaks between words or sentences or paragraphs. In fact it was also written in capitals. We can get an idea of the overall effect by imagining reading a Bible printed like this:

NOWONTHATSAMEDAYTWOOFTHEMWERE-
GOINGTOAVILLAGE . . .

There are also no such conventions as bold or italic or under-lining for emphasis or subtitles or section headings. The obvious problem with this way of writing which strikes us, then, is how could a New Testament author particularly emphasize a point? How they make sure a reader noted that here was a major turning point or a key moment in the story? We might use a subtitle, or a larger font, or put it in bold text. The equivalent in the first century was to build literary structures into the text.

For instance, you could write with a certain rhythm, so that as one read along they would notice that the author was high-lighting something (rather in the way that Shakespeare's plays often have rhyming couplets at the end of a scene, almost as a coded way of pointing out that the scene was about to change). Or you could repeat a key point twice in similar words: a device known as parallelism. This is very common in, for example, the Old Testament book of Proverbs. When you read 'My child, be attentive to my wisdom; incline your ear to my understanding' (Proverbs 5.1), both halves of the verse are saying the same thing, as a way of emphasizing the point being made.

The chiasm was simply a slightly more complex structure along the same lines: a short section of text which hinges or pivots around a central moment, and which pairs off elements of the story before and after that central moment. The key point of the chiasm was often to show just what a difference the central moment made. Of course there is a certain creative act of judgement in seeing a chiasm in the text: not all interpreters of the New Testament will agree on whether it is 'really' there, but perhaps this is not as significant as one might think at first. A more modest claim would simply be that such an observation can be a helpful way of looking at a text even if it is not necessarily the 'right' way of describing that text.

In this particular case, Green's suggested chiasm for Luke 24 seems to fit well enough, and it pivots around the central affirmation that Jesus is alive. In other words: the claim that Jesus is alive (and note that it is presented in v. 23 as a report to be considered rather than as an emphatic conclusion) is the key to seeing how the passage pulls together all that it is saying. To be precise: that Jesus is alive is the key difference between summarizing 'these things' and *interpreting* them.

Before we come on to the word 'interpreted' in v. 27, there are some other things that we can say about Luke 24, which draw us into the theological significance of the story. We might note that in v. 19 the travelling companions describe Jesus as 'a prophet mighty in deed and word'. Luke is fond of this way of describing Jesus: Acts 1.1, which refers back explicitly to the Gospel of Luke, takes up that Gospel by saying that it was about 'all that Jesus did and taught from the beginning' (although the translation is debatable here, but it does not affect this point). The combination of saying and doing, which are really two ways of performing acts of any kind, occurs also in the important story in Luke 4 where Jesus preaches in the synagogue at Nazareth, the real start of his public ministry according to Luke. There his 'gracious words' cause amazement, while at the same time he expects his listeners to challenge him to perform the 'deeds' which he had previously done elsewhere.

What then is the significance of Jesus being described as a 'prophet mighty in deed and in word'? In Acts 7.22 Luke reports Stephen, in his speech to the Jewish council in Jerusalem, describing Moses as 'powerful in his words and deeds'. Elsewhere in Acts 3.22 Peter thinks back to Moses and remembers the words of Deuteronomy 18.18 where a prophet like Moses is promised. For us to understand this we need to realize that Moses plays a role in the understanding of the Old Testament which is quite unique.

The so-called 'five books of Moses', from Genesis to Deuteronomy, were known as the *torah*, and formed a foundation document for Israel's faith. This was the basis around which all of the rest of 'the Scriptures' (in other words, the Old Testament as we would call it today) were built. All the Scriptures would have been taken seriously as a word from God, but still the *torah* always played the foundational role.

We may rightly interpret the word *torah* today as 'law', and indeed many do speak of 'the law' as a shorthand for these five books, but we must recognize that *torah* is so much more than what we tend to mean by 'law', as we shall see in the next chapter. Through the *torah*, Moses would still speak to the attentive Jewish believer at the time of Jesus. What are now typically called 'history books' in the Old Testament (Joshua, Judges, etc.) were then known as 'the prophets', and thus when Jesus begins with 'Moses and all the prophets' in Luke 24.27 he is basically interpreting all of Scripture as it then stood.

We also need to see that in describing Jesus as a prophet

mighty in deed and word, Luke is expecting his readers to pick up an echo of Moses. Here is the one who is fulfilling the role of the long-expected prophet of Deuteronomy 18. Luke is not saying, 'Jesus is that new Moses'. Rather he has in his mind the kinds of ways in which first-century Jewish believers would have been accustomed to think of Moses: as an authoritative figure, a prophetic figure, a mediator of the presence of God to the people and so forth. And then in describing Jesus as an authoritative figure, a prophet, and a mediator of God's presence, Luke is inviting his readers to see that Jesus fits as a 'new Moses' figure, which would have been understood to be a claim about Jesus' unique position and role in God's work.

This kind of 'old and new' approach is quite typical of biblical thinking. The point is that the writer takes a familiar way of looking at something well known, and uses it to describe something less well known. 'You all know about Moses and how we understand him in such and such a way,' the argument might run, 'well, now I am going to describe Jesus in the same way.' The writer avoids saying 'Jesus is Moses', or, to use a similar example, 'Jesus is Elijah' (compare Matthew 11.14 and John 1.21, referring back to Malachi 4.5), but the conclusion is supposed to be obvious, if you have eyes to see it. This way of thinking is probably also one of the ways to understand the New Testament portrayal of Jesus as God: typically for first-century monotheistic Jewish believers, the New Testament writers are very reluctant to say 'Jesus is God', a point which can cause some puzzlement or confusion today if we simply expect the New Testament to say what we want to know, rather than listening to it on its own terms. Instead, we find this type of argument: we all know that God has always been described in certain ways, and now we describe Jesus in the same ways (e.g. 'always present', as in Matthew 28.20, or able to forgive sins, as in Mark 2.1–12). The conclusion is left for the reader to draw. But there is only one conclusion which fits:

talk about Jesus is talk about God. Similarly here in Luke 24. Luke leaves us to draw our own conclusion: Jesus is the one greater than Moses who was prophesied and was eagerly expected. He is a 'new Moses' figure.

This kind of theological significance, seeing in Luke 24.19 the drawing of lines of connection between Jesus and Moses, is part of the sensitivity to reading the story which we should be trying to develop as we work with its texture and structure and start to see what we are supposed to be looking for. It will elude us for as long as we see the goal of biblical interpretation as the extraction of the one right meaning from the text. Biblical interpretation is more subtle than that: it is tied up with the long, slow skill of learning to think theologically.

Which leads us on to a final point from the Emmaus story, and in its way one of the most important observations about biblical interpretation which we can make. It involves Luke 24.27, a verse which reads:

> Then beginning with Moses and all the prophets,
> he *interpreted* to them
> the things about himself in all the Scriptures

(The emphasis, of course, is added). This word 'interpreted' is the normal Greek word for 'interpreted': *diermēneusen*. The *di-* prefix simply indicates its particular tense, and disguises the fact that the word concerned is *hermēneuein*, to interpret or to explain. This is the word that gives us the modern English word 'hermeneutics', the art of interpretation or of explanation and understanding. This is not a technical word that Luke is using, but is simply the normal word for what he wants to say: Jesus *interpreted* the Scriptures. It is also worth noting that this is the only place in the New Testament where this particular word occurs, although this does not mean that the rest of the New Testament is unconcerned with interpretation.

'Hermeneutics' has become a fashionable word these days for what used to be called simply 'biblical interpretation'. In fact, the way it is often used, there seems to be no difference between it and 'interpretation', and I have some sympathy with those who feel that it is itself a piece of jargon designed to obscure what should be very straightforward: the reading and understanding of the Bible. It is sometimes even suggested that the Church seemed to manage perfectly well without hermeneutics until a few years ago, so why now is there the need for so much to be written and said about 'biblical hermeneutics'?

Several things could be said at this point. As noted in the introduction, 'hermeneutics' is actually not just interpretation, but it is the evaluation of interpretation too: the whole question of what it means to understand and explain a text and what criteria there are for evaluating it. But more to the point, the 'straightforward' meaning of the biblical text is often a way of saying 'straightforward for me', and does not appear equally straightforward for everyone. In fact, this is precisely one of the issues in Luke 24: all the disciples could read the Scriptures and see what they said, but the 'interpretation' which Jesus is about to offer is not one with which they would have been familiar. It is helpful to realize that when we are talking about hermeneutics in connection with the Bible, we are standing in a line of tradition which goes back to Jesus himself on the Emmaus road, conducting a Bible study which it would have been a great privilege to attend, but which Luke evidently did not consider it appropriate to summarize at this point.

Notice what is happening here. Recall that in the story as we have studied it, there was a general agreement on the 'facts', that, for example, the tomb was empty. It was the interpretation of those facts which was causing the trouble. What made the difference? Not new and better facts that underlined the first set of facts. Facts were not hard currency, such that if you had enough of them they added up to an interpretation, and indeed they still do not work that way. What actually made the difference was having Jesus give his hearers a way of looking at the Old Testament Scriptures which showed them that what had taken place in Jerusalem was after all what should have been anticipated. It should have been what Jewish believers were hoping and waiting for rather than a dramatic reversal which called into question all the various hopes around at that time, hopes for a Messiah, for vindication, for God to prove that, somehow, God's side was the right side to be on.

The two travellers on the road to Emmaus recognize Jesus when he eats with them, since the breaking of bread was in a sense a way of using any meal as a chance to remember Jesus' instruction to remember him in bread and wine. Their eyes now opened to the biblical text, finally the scales fall away and they see who Jesus is. But note that it was only in walking and talking with Jesus that they first had their eyes opened to the biblical text. Their understanding of Jesus gave them access to an understanding of Scripture. Their understanding of Scripture enabled them to understand Jesus. It is not one or the other, not even necessarily first one and then the other also, but rather the two together, each feeding into and supporting the other (see Fig. 1).

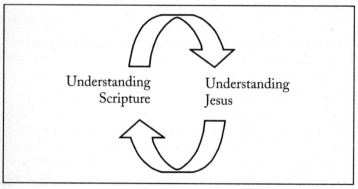

Fig. 1 Understanding Jesus and understanding Scripture

Thus we have a kind of 'circle' of understanding, more usually called a 'hermeneutical circle': in the words of Joel Green, 'What has happened with Jesus can be understood only in the light of the Scriptures, yet the Scriptures themselves can be understood only in the light of what has happened with Jesus. These two are mutually informing.'[2] But the word 'circle', perhaps by connotation with the idea of a 'vicious circle', tends to give the impression that our interpretation is consigned to go around in circles never getting anywhere, and so it is often argued that we should call this a 'hermeneutical spiral': each time we go around the circle we get more out of it.

Our reading of Scripture deepens as our relationship with Jesus deepens. Our relationship with Jesus becomes more subtle, more profound, as our ability to see him as the fulfilment of all of Scripture increases. In this sense, we never arrive at the point where we have finished reading the Bible. Obviously, we can start at the beginning of Genesis and read right through to the end of Revelation, although this is a daunting prospect and often more mechanical than motivational. But every time we come to a familiar passage later in time, we come to it as a different person, changed in who we are, and thus changed in our reading of the passage, which then in turn challenges and changes our relationship with who Jesus is.

Rather as the fact of the empty tomb required a framework before it could begin to make sense, the framework provided by the dawning realization that Jesus was alive, and that this was all according to the Scriptures, so the bare text before us, as we read the Bible, desperately needs a framework before it can begin to make sense to us. How many of us are familiar with the experience of patiently reading a Bible passage, or hearing one read out in church, and at the end of it having not a clue as to what has actually been said? The words go in, and we may even know the broad outline of what is being said, but the sense of the passage eludes us completely. When this

21

happens, as it often does, what we need is a framework, something other than yet more words to explain the first set of words, but some kind of vantage point, some perspective, some 'a-ha!' insight which makes us see that *these* words are pointing to *this way* of looking at things.

What then makes the difference between reading and interpreting the Bible? In Luke 24, the difference is Jesus. One can read the New Testament for many reasons, but for Christians concerned about the nature of God and what sort of life God would ask us to live, we read the New Testament not just as words on a page, but as Christian Scripture. Indeed, some have said that to read the Bible as 'Scripture' is already to offer an interpretative framework, and a theological one at that. It is to say that God is involved in the interpretative task. To read the New Testament as Christian Scripture is to see Jesus in the light of the Scriptures, and the Scriptures in the light of Jesus. It is to bring Bible reading into the heart of what it means to be spiritual and vice versa.

There are a lot of ways that this point needs to be clarified and handled carefully, not least in trying to link the idea that Jesus stands at the centre of all Bible reading with the traditional Christian theological claim that God is a trinity of Father, Son and Holy Spirit at one and the same time. This is not the place to discuss the Trinity, but suffice to say that where Luke 24 takes us as far as 'Christ-centred' Bible reading, this need not stop us, on other grounds, developing a fully trinitarian Bible reading to develop this insight, and not to undermine it. We would also need to reconsider, if what has been said so far is true, just what we meant in the first place by 'facts', which is one reason why I occasionally retain 'scare quotes' around the word, to indicate that a fact is not always a fact, depending on who is looking at what, and who is trying to say what. All of this is the concern of those interested in 'theological hermeneutics', the forbidding label for the basic issue of how to read the Bible theologically.

For us it is enough to note that the simple attempt to read the Emmaus story in Luke 24 led us straight to theological questions as it introduced us to the task of reading the Bible in its theological context. Without these questions, we might well return from the seven-mile walk to Emmaus every bit as confused and disheartened as we began it, only now we would be worn out into the bargain. With the disciples, we are drawn in, eyes opened, to seeing that all the Scriptures (v. 27) point to Jesus, and that our growth as Christians depends on both our experience of Jesus *and* our experience of Scripture, not just one or the other. Far from being worn out by the walk, we would only wish that the seven miles had been longer, and that we might have got to overhear more of what Jesus said on the journey, as we began to grasp what it meant to read the Bible in its theological context.

♦ 2 ♦

Reading the Bible as a Historical Book: The Pharisee and the Tax Collector

Luke 18.9–14

♦

You believe that . . .
>. . . the Scriptures are the word of God.
>. . . they apply to all of life.
>. . . it is important to interpret them properly.
>. . . God still speaks through his Scriptures today.
>. . . God's word is for everyone, even those who do
>   not realize it.

Who are you?

Perhaps you are an evangelical. As you read down the list you find yourself strongly agreeing with all these statements: this could be part of your own outlook on the Bible. You might even go further, and argue that these are the precise points at which today's Christian needs to stand firm against the tide of woolly-minded loose thinking so characteristic of other branches of the Church. Well, you may be glad to know, you are not alone.

You may not be so glad to realize who your fellow defenders of the faith are, agreeing with all those points as they read down the list: they are the Pharisees, those well-known heroes of the New Testament. Can that be right? This sets us off on the historical trail which we shall be exploring in this chapter.

The story of the Pharisee and the tax collector (or better:

toll collector) is a short parable told by Jesus to some who trusted that they were righteous, in the words of Luke 18.9. The basics of the story are simple, and well known in that 'well-known' sort of way which tends to obscure what is actually going on. Two men go up to the temple to pray, and the Pharisee congratulates himself on all the good things he does, while the toll collector simply asks for God to be merciful to him, since he is a sinner. The second one, and not the first, goes home justified, which, we may note, is basically the same word as 'righteous' in v. 9.

Who are we as we read this story? Clearly not the Pharisee, who slots neatly into our 'bad guy' role. We are the 'sinner', not perhaps a toll collector, but at least someone who knows the right answer: that we are righteous by the grace of God and not because we have impressed God in the first place. The moral is obvious: Pharisees get what is coming to them. Do not be like them. Confess your sin instead, and God will welcome you in.

There is, of course, a profound half-truth in this, which is what ensures that this interpretation endures and is so often the one which is preached from this passage. The truth is that the confession that I am a sinner is precisely what qualifies me to receive this 'righteousness' which God offers, although at this point we have done no work in deciding what such a concept as 'righteousness' could really be. The problem is rather with the other half of the interpretation, which suggests that we are not supposed to be like Pharisees, who are basically seen as religious hypocrites. Here is where we need to begin to do some serious historical homework.

For many Bible readers today, the Pharisees have a walk-on part, existing solely to provide sermon illustrations for Jesus, typifying all that is wrong with the religious establishment, of which we are proud (in a humble sort of way) not to be a part. A moment's reflection should indicate that the whole picture is bound to be a lot more complex than this. Who were the Pharisees? Who did *they* think they were, for instance? What would they have said were their aims and driving ambitions? What does the word 'Pharisee' mean anyway? In a flash of inspiration we consider turning back to the Old Testament to see something of their background and origin, and there we meet with a puzzle. In the Old Testament the Pharisees are conspicuous by their absence. So where did they come from? Who are these people?

The word 'Pharisee' appears to derive from the Hebrew *parash*, and means 'one who separates'. Thus a Pharisee is a separated person, but separated from what? To answer this we need to know something of the so-called 'intertestamental period' (sometimes abbreviated to ITP), the time between the Old Testament story which more or less finishes with the restoration of Jerusalem under Ezra and Nehemiah in the fifth and fourth centuries BC and the arrival of Jesus. The broad plot outline of the Old Testament takes us from Egypt through the Exodus into the promised land, through the turbulent centuries of Israel's self-governance under Saul, David, Solomon and succeeding kings, the split of the kingdom into two, and the eventual exile of both halves, the Southern Kingdom finally falling to the Babylonians in about 587 BC. The return to Jerusalem under the Persian king Cyrus was led by Ezra, and the city of Jerusalem was largely restored under Nehemiah. And there the story appears to end, with the obvious question being: what happened next? Do things just carry on in largely mundane ways until the dawn of the New Testament? Was it, in a sense, happy ever after once Ezra and Nehemiah had done their work?

No it was not. The trials and difficulties, as well as the successes and victories, of the intertestamental period rival anything in the David and Solomon era, but since they are not in either half of the Bible they are much less well known. I choose my words advisedly here, because the place where these stories can be found is in the apocrypha, a collection of books occasionally included in some Bibles, and then appropriately printed between the two testaments. In particular the book of 1 Maccabees tells the story of the Maccabean family resisting the then-ruling Seleucid dynasty and restoring the temple sacrifices after the temple had been the subject of attack by the Seleucid ruler Antiochus Epiphanes IV in 167 BC. (The account of the rededication of the temple is in 1 Maccabees 4.36–61. The festival which remembers this, and which continues to this day, is *Hanukkah*, or the 'feast of dedication', which is the feast occurring in John 10.22, another New Testament reference which cannot be understood from the Old Testament alone.)

Most scholars agree that this whole period of intense persecution from 167 to 164 BC is the occasion for the later, somewhat bizarre chapters of the book of Daniel with all their talk of the 'abomination that causes desolation' (Daniel 11.31; 12.11) occurring on the temple site. One of the reasons why Daniel is written in the unfamiliar style of 'apocalyptic' is that it is written at just such a time of persecution and threat to the people of God (a theme we will revisit when we consider the book of Revelation later). One of the fundamental claims of the Maccabean revolt, of the desire to reclaim for God what had become compromised and defiled, was that a new obedience to God was required which would not tolerate any form of compromise. Here we need to see especially that the typically modern dissection of life into separate compartments such as spiritual, religious, social, political, personal, etc., would not have made any sense at this time. Life was a whole, and if one belonged to God then every aspect of life must be dedicated to God.

It is against this background that the Pharisees developed. They were dedicated to the written *torah*, but by this time the

27

written *torah* was continually being reinterpreted for new situations which it had not originally been intended for, and this on-going work of interpretation had given rise to a body of oral tradition which would subsequently grow into the massive collection of rabbinic writings that we possess today. To put the point in its simplest form: the Pharisees represent an attempt to adapt Judaism to a new situation, and to avoid the mistakes of earlier generations who had made peace with ruling empires only to see their own worship and integrity compromised by those in power.

The Israel of the New Testament was under Roman rule, through a system of local rulers called tetrarchs, a word which originally meant 'ruler of a fourth part', but came to refer to the various delegated rulers of Israel and the surrounding area, for example, Philip in Luke 3.1. It found itself in a complex world of political and social relationships where the Pharisees stand in basic opposition to those among the Jewish people who sought cooperation with Rome as the way forward. All of this, we might note, is immediately relevant to reading the New Testament in today's equally complex social and political world, where Christians differ so widely in their attitudes to the role of the state in public and church life.

To many in Israel at the time, the Pharisees were threatening because they appeared to stand for all that was 'religiously correct', and yet they did it in unnerving and complicated ways which were bound up with their ongoing interpretation of *torah*. Perhaps, after all, they were right, and perhaps too many people simply dealt with the conflicts between *torah* and society by ignoring or spiritualizing away the awkward details of Moses' words. If you are among the crowds listening to the parables in Luke 18, you are probably thinking that it would of course be great to be as dedicated to God as the Pharisees are, but you do not have the time for it, since dealing with all the requirements of daily life leaves you worn out enough as it is.

What are we to make of this? The first point to make is that our historical homework immediately paints a much more sympathetic picture of the Pharisees than the New Testament does. Second, if we have begun to understand why the Pharisees thought the way they did, then we will notice that they faced a very familiar issue: everything they did came from a love for God, but all too easily they crossed over a fine line and ended up thinking that they were all right (or all righteous?) with God *because* they were doing all these things. At this point they would lose sight of the gracious basis on which God had invited his people into the covenant in the first place.

The question persists, then, as to why Jesus is so forthright: 'Beware of the yeast of the Pharisees, that is, their hypocrisy' (Luke 12.1). In one of the most damning passages of the entire New Testament, Matthew has Jesus saying, 'Woe to you, scribes and Pharisees, hypocrites! For you tithe mint, dill, and cummin, and have neglected the weightier matters of the law: justice and mercy and faith' (Matthew 23.23). The Pharisees according to Jesus are hypocritical, although we should note that he is not saying that it was a mistake to tithe herbs, only that other matters were neglected which were 'weightier', that is, which had more significant consequences.

To hold these observations together with our more sympathetic picture of the Pharisees requires us to know a little more about the Jewish world that lies behind the Gospels. Most scholars pick out four separate groups of the time, and then observe that the vast majority of Jewish people were not members of any of them, they were 'the people of the land' (the *am-ha-aretz*) whose daily lives revolved around work and subsistence, with only the Sabbath set aside as a day when the work could stop. Of these four groups, the Pharisees are the ones we read most about in the New Testament.

The Sadducees, about whom relatively little is known, occur in some Gospel stories, notably the passage where they construct the unlikely scenario about one bride for seven brothers who all die one after the other (Luke 20.27–40 and also in Matthew and Mark). They are not interested in the pastoral impact of this on the poor woman, but on the technical issues this raises concerning who would be married to whom in the life to come. The point: such a case seems to make a nonsense of the whole idea of the resurrection life. Indeed the Sadducees are mainly known today for what they did not believe rather than what they did: 'The Sadducees say that there is no resurrection, or angel, or spirit; but the Pharisees acknowledge all three' (Acts 23.8). This is an important clue to the reason for the Pharisees turning up so often in the New Testament.

We should briefly mention the other two types of people. First, there were the 'Essenes', noted for their separatist existence out in the hills surrounding Israel. Little was known about them until the discovery of the so-called Dead Sea Scrolls in a cave at Qumran, along the Western edge of the Dead Sea, between 1947 and 1956. There are, in all likelihood, no examples of Essenes in the New Testament, not even John the Baptist, whose wild eccentricity and desert existence once made him a prime candidate for this identification; but the evidence for this is inconclusive. Second, there were the Zealots, of whom Simon is identified as one in Luke 6.15, and perhaps the 'bandits' on the cross (Mark 15.27) are also examples. There was a well-known Zealot uprising in AD 6, mentioned in Acts 5.36–7, but mentioned somewhat problematically since Luke's account of who was involved (or at least his report of Gamaliel's account of who was involved) does not fit any known historical information we have. This kind of discrepancy excites some people very much, and in the care and attention devoted to 'resolving' this issue we return to the spirit of the Pharisees, for whom this would have been precisely the kind of issue to cause considerable debate.

None of these other groups really demand much attention

in the New Testament, so why the Pharisees? We are now in a position to answer. It is because they are so close. Their concern for God and for the proper response to God's word is fundamentally what God would have wanted. Their passionate desire to do what was right was in itself wonderful, but in their concern for demarcating precisely what was right and wrong they betrayed something more important: an ability to focus on what was truly central to the life of faith and obedience. Jesus was so hard on the Pharisees because in their effort to clarify the right way to God they were in fact blocking the doorway to the kingdom of heaven, and nobody else could get past. They had their faces pressed up against the glass, and nobody else could see in. Jesus would have been delighted to welcome them in, and indeed he eats with them and generally mixes with them in the Gospels, but they in turn drive others away with their relentless attention to the detailed interpretation of the *torah* and its oral traditions.

We do not need to rely on this kind of broad-brushstroke reconstruction of what must have been the problem, because we actually have considerable documentation of some of the Jewish interpretations of the law during that period. The oral traditions surrounding the *torah* are written down for us in a collection from around the end of the second century AD entitled the *Mishnah*, while an enormous sprawling rabbinic commentary on it, known as the *Talmud*, occupies many large volumes. (It is true that these sources need careful historical handling, and that they tend to represent only certain lines of thought in first-century Judaism, mainly the more liberal tendencies which survived into the second century when these books were written down, but this need not unduly concern us here.) The most celebrated saying in the *Mishnah* is:

Moses received Torah at Sinai and handed it on to Joshua, Joshua to elders, and elders to prophets.

And prophets handed it on to the men of the
   great assembly.
They said three things:
   'Be prudent in judgement.
   'Raise up many disciples.
   'Make a fence for the Torah.'[1]

Here we find the chain of tradition stretching back to Moses,
the ongoing work of wise discernment entrusted to that tradition and, in the final command, the idea of 'making a fence
for the Torah'. What does this mean? It basically requires
the erection of a 'safety zone' around the actual requirements
of *torah*, so that even if one transgresses the safety zone, the
commands of *torah* themselves are not breached.

For example, one must not work on the Sabbath: this much
is more than clear in the *torah* (in addition to the well-known
'fourth commandment' there are such unequivocal passages as
Exodus 31.12–17). In Numbers 15.32 the Israelites find a man
gathering sticks on the Sabbath: after some confusion it is
concluded that this breaks Sabbath too. Since transporting
objects from one place to another is work, the idea becomes
that one must not carry things around on the Sabbath. But
then, what if a beggar approaches your house with a begging
bowl and thrusts it into your hand. Can you hand it back to
him, even if it means transporting an object on the Sabbath?
Well, it depends on who initiates the movement, or on
whether a greater act of generosity is being performed in feeding the beggar; and in various circumstances one person or
the other, or both, are exempt from violating the Sabbath.
Confused? Tractate *Shabbat* 1.1 will sort it out for you in two
cases, which are four, for both the one inside a property and
the one outside the property. The fact that this single issue in
itself ends up comprising fifteen sub-points indicates the
inevitable complexity of this line of thinking. If you do in fact

manage to tithe all your herbs correctly then one thing is certain: you will be busy. Arguably so busy that you will never get round to weightier matters.

But all of this is an exercise in hedge-building, and the real problem comes when you spot your neighbour not exactly breaking *torah*, but breaking the hedge around the *torah*, and you fail to spot this crucial difference. The *torah* does not require fasting twice a week, but to do so certainly fulfils what it does require. What now will the Pharisee in Luke 18 say when his neighbour fasts only as often as *torah* itself requires?

And what now will we say? We who take God's word seriously and are concerned to construct our own hedges around it lest we might transgress God's commands. We who know what we are doing and know that what we are doing is right in God's eyes, whether it be going to church every Sunday, giving to charity, avoiding stealing and adultery, driving always within the speed limit, generously leaving a tip at the end of a meal in a restaurant or rightly paying airport tax to fly out of Heathrow but refusing to pay 'bribes' in far-flung cafés and airports, to take a select list which would have gone down very well indeed with our Pharisee in Luke 18. He is still standing and praying in the middle of the temple for all who will hear him, and in this, we should note, he is not unusual. This is not a strange kind of pride in being spiritual, but is the kind of prayer we find in the *Talmud*, where the rabbis taught that a man might pray, as he leaves worship:

> I give thanks to Thee, O Lord my God, that . . . Thou hast not set my portion with those who sit in (street) corners, for I rise early and they rise early, but I rise early for words of Torah and they rise early for frivolous talk . . . I run to the life of the future world and they run to the pit of destruction.[2]

Our Pharisee is simply giving thanks for the very things we would think it appropriate to give thanks for.

We read Luke 18.9–14, six short verses which see the Pharisees get their just deserts, and we think that this is the way it is supposed to be: the self-righteous brought down low and the lowly lifted up. And this is true, but we have read it from the wrong position, since now the parable has simply confirmed what we already thought:

> The parable is usually 'understood' as a reassuring moral tale which condemns the kind of Pharisaism that everyone already wishes to avoid. A parable which originally had the function of unsettling the hearer and overturning his values now serves to confirm him in the values which he already has.[3]

And thus the parable, if we have now learned to read it in its historical context, should unsettle us greatly. Commentators have tried very hard to worry away at v. 14, where the toll collector went home justified (*dikaiōmenos*, the word which comes from the same root as 'righteousness' in Greek, *dikaiosunē*) and have said that here we surely do not have the full-blown Christian doctrine of justification, with all the staggering implications this would have for, of all people, a toll collector. Toll collectors were as near to the bottom of the pile as made no difference: they made their living charging extra on the Roman tolls which were in place at just about every border crossing in the area, and thus they not only annoyed everyone who tried to travel anywhere, but they served as a constant reminder of the much-loathed Roman governance which lay at the root of so much of Israel's trouble in the first place.

If these kind of people are now going to get justified, and *torah*-abiding religious leaders, the upright pillars of society, are going to be thrown out into the cold, then something is happening which will do more than just annoy those who are doing all right by this present system. This is the kind of offensive and subversive teaching which could get you killed. And on reflection it seems hardly likely that anyone is really going to kill a teacher whose basic moral point was 'don't be like one of those hypocrite bad guys, but look out for the poor good guys'. That is a message that Hollywood, for instance, would have little trouble portraying. But a gospel message . . . the one that comes into focus when we read the Bible in its historical context, is an altogether different proposition, and anyone taking the Bible seriously as a word from God, and attempting to interpret it faithfully for today's world, needs to think twice before responding to Luke 18.9–14 by praying 'Dear God, I thank you that I am not like the Pharisee'.

For it is in returning from the detailed world of historical reconstruction, of learning to see the Pharisees and every other historical aspect of the New Testament world in the right focus, and with the right associations, that we allow the biblical text to speak in the voice which it intended. We may want to defend our own approach to Scripture on the grounds that it is God's word, and therefore needs to be interpreted to cover every eventuality, and we may start to suppose that this requires copious lists of rules and regulations about what is and is not permitted, and we may do all of this thinking that this is no more than simple obedience to the task of taking the Bible seriously, but once we have done our homework we realize that this, for all its obvious merits and good intentions, is to stand in the shoes (or sandals) of the Pharisee. And we may have all kinds of good reasons for distrusting today's equivalents of the toll collectors, who perhaps make money out of the National Lottery, or over-charging on simple car repairs because the insurance will pay, or working for newspapers which enjoy lampooning Christianity as a ridiculous and hypo-critical bunch of people trying to impose moral standards on people, but when such people ask the God of mercy to have mercy, and acknowledge their sin and ask for it to be washed away, then God will indeed wash it away, and send them home justified. And every time we think we are nearer the first of these two stereotypes, then we should watch out, for we are likely to be brought down low, and every time we recognize ourselves in the second, we should rejoice, because we might get to go home righteous.

One church home group which I attended had in it a woman who worked at the local tax office, sending out reminders to people who had not paid their taxes. It was always wonderful to read a parable like this one in a group which included her, especially if she had come along after a hard day telephoning people who had repaid her courtesy with various bursts of rudeness and insults. She liked the fact that she got to be justified in this parable, although she struggled with some of the other New Testament passages which left tax collectors more conspicuously on the outside.

The good news for her, and for those like her, is that doing our historical homework shows clearly *why* the tax collectors were ahead of the Pharisees at the end of the parable in Luke 18: that it was not just a happy coincidence which would brighten the day of a modern tax office worker, but was an outworking of the logic of God's gracious gospel, clearly if outrageously explained by Jesus 2000 years ago, and understandable today by reading the Bible in its historical context.

♦ 3 ♦

Reading the Bible as a Literary Work: Luke's 'Orderly Account'

Luke 9.51

♦

Whatever else it is, the Gospel of Luke is a story, or a narrative. How should we read a story? Most people know that a good way to read a story is to start at the beginning, go on until the end, and then stop. Most people who read the Bible probably know this too, but in practice they hardly ever do it. We can of course see why this is: most of us do not read 2000-year-old stories most of the time, and thus the amount of background detail which we do not really have a clue about is unusually high when we read a story like Luke's Gospel, although in theory this is no different from reading *Pride and Prejudice* and needing to know about social conventions in early nineteenth-century England. Similarly, most of the stories we read do not come as part of an authoritative book, and while the nature of biblical authority is always hard to define precisely (as we shall see in Chapter 6), it must have something to do with making an impact on the way we live. But how? Here is where a biblical story really needs to be handled as a story.

Anything plucked out of its story setting (or its 'narrative context', as critics like to say) may set off quite inappropriate lines of thinking. Here is Luke 10.4: 'Carry no purse, no bag, no sandals; and greet no one on the road.' The first part of this need not suggest to us that purses or wallets are 'unbiblical', any more than the second part is a justification for the typical modern British lack of courtesy as one walks down the High Street. Equally, when we arrive at Luke 22.36, 'now the one who has a purse must take it' this is not a 'contradiction' of the previous passage, and the startling conclusion to the verse, 'the one who has no sword must sell his cloak and buy one', should not draw the unwary into investing heavily in shares in sword manufacturing companies.

Just as the previous chapter started with a short passage from Luke and then took a lengthy historical detour in order to come back and read it afresh, so this chapter will begin with what looks like a particularly uninteresting verse tucked away in the middle of the Gospel, and then try to build up a narrative framework around it to give us new ways of looking at Luke. The focus here is on the literary features of the text: reading the Bible as a literary work and with awareness of what kinds of questions this raises for us.

We should note right at the outset that literary questions are raised for us by Luke, in the preface to his two-volume work (Luke–Acts), when he gives us his explanation for what he has written, namely, 'an orderly account of the events that have been fulfilled among us' (Luke 1.1 and also v. 3). Luke's work is not the breathless note-taking of Mark's Gospel, which rushes from story to story with barely a pause for breath, but is the considered work of an editor (or 'redactor' as biblical scholars like to say) who has read all the sources and is here compiling an 'orderly account'. But which 'order'? And how does Luke put his account in order?

We can start to respond to this by comparing the Gospels of Matthew, Mark and Luke, commonly called the three Synoptic Gospels, with 'synoptic' here meaning 'seen together', and thus all covering basically the same material, or all 'seeing' the same thing. When we cross-compare them we soon notice that the order of the events within the three Gospels varies considerably. Luke's order does not therefore necessarily correspond closely to the 'historical order' of events, or if it does then Matthew and Mark do not. In other words, Luke has other reasons than historical accuracy for putting his account in the order he does, and that is what we shall pursue here. Basically we want to know what *Luke* meant to say by telling his story *this* way, rather than what Jesus meant, or what necessarily happened. This is known technically as 'redaction criticism', since it asks about the intentions of the 'redactor' (or editor) but my own view is that it is often simply the commonsense asking of good literary questions which is all part of how we generally think about stories, and on the whole we shall avoid talking about 'redaction' wherever possible.

The verse we shall begin with is a brief description of Jesus in Luke 9.51, which the NRSV translates, accurately, as 'When the days drew near for him to be taken up, he set his face to go to Jerusalem'. This may not seem like much to go on, but let us see where it leads.

Luke 9.51 is a 'getting underway' verse. It is like that part of the story which says 'they loaded up the car and set off'. Maybe it is of no significance at all, except that Luke several times stops and makes this kind of observation. Consider how he reports Jesus' words in chapter 13: 'I am casting out demons and performing cures today and tomorrow, and on the third day I must finish my work . . . I must be on my way, because it is impossible for a prophet to be killed outside of Jerusalem' (vv. 32–3). In 17.11 we find 'On the way to Jerusalem Jesus was going through the region between Samaria and Galilee'. At first sight, if we consult a map at this point, this does not seem the quickest route to take, except that direct travel through Samaria would have been quite exceptional at the time, with Samaritans being so severely disliked by the Jewish population at large. Even though the 'parable of the good Samaritan' is fresh in our memories at this point in the Gospel, perhaps Luke is simply acknowledging that Jesus took the standard

Samaritan-avoiding route. Nevertheless, there is something interesting going on here, since back in 9.52 Jesus *was* going through Samaria. It is hard to avoid the conclusion that if Jesus were simply engaged in transit to Jerusalem there would have been quicker ways of going about his business.

In Luke 18.31, Jesus takes his disciples aside and says, 'See, we are going up to Jerusalem', and four verses later they are on their way, passing Jericho as they go. All these references to movement and purpose have led scholars to propose the name 'Luke's travel narrative' for this central section of the Gospel, or rather it has led many scholars this way, although some prefer 'Luke's central section', which is true enough, but nowhere near as interesting.

Once we start to think in terms of a 'travel narrative', we begin to notice all kinds of markers of movement. Indeed, to pick up the hints we had in Chapter 1 on the Emmaus story, the 'journey' theme is one of the ways Luke tells his overall story, and for good reason. We note that in 10.1, a verse which is obviously mainly about the sending out of the Seventy, Luke adds 'every town and place *where he himself intended to go*' (though admittedly Luke does not use italics, but then how could he . . . ?). In 10.38 they are going merrily on their way. In 13.22 Jesus goes through 'one town and village after another'. This whole theme is magnified in chapter 19, which begins in Jericho, noted in v. 11 as being 'near Jerusalem'. Of course whether one notes that Jericho is near Jerusalem or not tells us more about the one doing the noting than about the geographical locations involved: it is noted here because Jerusalem is looming into view in the (middle) distance. In v. 28 Jesus goes on up to Jerusalem, and soon he is drawing near to the city and then entering the temple. Time after time Luke points out Jesus' progress. Why?

One of the ways in which an author can highlight a major point in the narrative is by playing with the speed of the story.

On a very simple level this can be seen in Martin Kähler's delightful characterization of Mark's Gospel especially, but of all the Gospels, as 'passion narratives with extended introductions',[1] one of those great over-simplifications which captures a more important big picture than all the many details it omits. Since about half of Mark's Gospel is taken up with the passion narrative, clearly one of the great emphases of Mark is the story of the death of Jesus. The time spent in telling that part of the story is proportionately far greater than the time spent telling the rest of the (preceding) story. Likewise, Luke moves briskly through the stories of Jesus' birth and childhood, and slows the pace down when he arrives at the synagogue in Nazareth so that we are enabled to hear the words of Jesus as he preaches from Isaiah. The most obvious of these 'slowing down' moments occurs here in chapter 19 as we finally arrive at Jerusalem, the city which has been in view ever since 9.51. We shall reconsider shortly just why there is no obvious moment of 'closure' in the story at the point where Jesus does finally arrive there.

It is hard to capture this kind of 'pacing' in a narrative in our world of short hyper-text links and sound-bite attention spans. Films compress entire novels into two hours of screen time, but in their own way have their own devices to tell you how fast time is going: the love story which is established in painstaking detail, and then several weeks or months pass in a few moments while music plays over the dialogue and we cut in rapid transition through a representative selection of shots of the happy couple engaged in day-to-day pursuits, laughing and grinning their way through both their relationship and narrative time. We pick up the story again as the music fades and we refocus on the next episode to be told at normal speed. Sometimes we achieve the same effect by having a narrator's voice superimposed on the story: 'And it came to pass, in that time, that a great famine came upon the land . . .'. The narrator speaks in a kind of omniscient 'view from nowhere' voice. In so doing, the author picks us up, redirects our attention to a new section of the story, and then leaves us to it again.

That is exactly what happens in Luke 9.51. We are reading happily along about the story of the transfiguration, that odd moment where Jesus meets with Moses and Elijah up a mountain, and then there is various business concerning demons and an exorcism, when suddenly, almost as clearly as the voice from the sky at Jesus' baptism, the voice of the narrator breaks in to make an announcement: 'When the days drew near . . .'. In fact, the Greek at this point becomes highly formal, just the kind of stilted announcer's voice which tells us (without any bold, italic or underlined font) that a new section of text is beginning. A bumpy, over-literal translation of the verse and the succeeding passage would give us this:

> [51]When drew near (in fulfilment) the days of his assumption and he set his face to go to Jerusalem. [52]And he sent messengers before his face. And, going, they entered into a Samaritan village to make it ready for him [53]but they did not receive him, because his face was going to Jerusalem . . . [56]They went to another village. [57]As they were going, in the way . . .

Any self-respecting English translation of this passage would rightly smooth a lot of this out, such as the repeated 'face', or the constant use of the verb 'to go' or 'going', and this is only fair for a translation which is setting its sights on the main picture of the story which we are in the middle of hearing. But in so doing we miss the deliberate slowing effect, the focus, the indication that here something new and important is happening.

What is the key to this strangely translated passage? The setting of one's face to a task is an idiom which still survives in

English today: the sense of purpose, resolution in the face of hardship and difficulty, and overall that sense of taking on a mission which is just what characterizes Jesus here. The 'going' is so obviously a feature that we should pause to consider just what it can indicate. It seems to highlight the 'journey' image which we noted above. It is worth looking at this in more detail.

In 9.57 Luke has Jesus and the disciples 'going along the road', and the word 'road' (*hodos*) is the same word which simply means 'way', as in 'they were going along the way'. It is no coincidence, then, that in the book of Acts, the title 'The Way' becomes a kind of label for the early Christian movement, still unformalized and known by many different labels, but in Acts 9.22; 19.9, 23; 22.4; 24.14, 22, it is 'The Way'. Clearly this sense of Christianity as 'the way' represents Christianity as a forward-moving way of living: life with a purpose, perhaps. It is captured particularly of Jesus in John 14.6 ('I am the way. . .' (*hodos*)). One of the things Luke seems to want to communicate is that the Christian life is itself like a journey. It is the following of Christ, not necessarily knowing where that journey will end, or at least not knowing all the places it will take in en route, but it is a dynamic experience, rather than a 'state' one enters. To be a Christian is not to arrive at some new place, but to embark on a new journey.

Luke highlights that journey in 9.57, and it is a journey *shown* by the way he tells the story rather than being explicitly what he says about what happened. In other words, it is a literary journey, doubtless with a historical backdrop, but that is not the focus. Again, we miss this if we insist on plucking out facts from what the biblical text *tells* us at any cost, in this case at the cost of letting the peculiar texture of this text *show* us the way.

Now that we have this journey in our sights, we need to be more specific about it, and in particular we must revisit the question of where Jesus is going. Two points will help us here. The first is to note more carefully the word used to initiate the journey description, where we read (back in 9.51 again) that what were drawing near were the days of Jesus' assumption (*analēmpsis*), or 'taking up'. Which taking up is this? It seems likely that the 'taking up' of Jesus in view here is his ascension, although arguably it could also be a word used to describe his death, raised up on the cross. A reason to prefer the 'ascension' view will become apparent in a moment.

Second, if Luke 9.51–6 is setting out the beginnings of a journey of major importance, then perhaps we should be looking for clues around this section of Luke as to where Jesus is said to be going. We know that Jerusalem is in view, but does Luke say anything else about this journey? If we then turn to the surrounding stories we will notice something about the way Luke tells the transfiguration story in chapter 9.

The transfiguration story is unusual, even by Gospel standards. Jesus meets with God on a mountain. In fact he meets with Moses and Elijah, with all the symbols of divine presence in place too (the dazzling white, the changed appearance, the glory, the voice from the cloud and so forth). The whole scene is reminiscent of Moses' various meetings with God up a mountain (the stories of Exodus 24 and 34) – not that anybody really believed that God was high up in the sky and thus that a mountain was a good way to get to him, but rather that here was a place set apart from the day-to-day cares of the world where one could make space for receiving from God. Perhaps Moses and Elijah symbolize the law and the prophets, although probably it is at least as significant that they both, in different ways, 'cheated' death: Moses with an unknown burial place, such that he was still present and still 'spoke' wherever *torah* was taken seriously, and Elijah with his chariots of fire, riding into a sunset whose details we shall pick up shortly.

This story (9.28–36) occurs also in Matthew 17.1–9 and

Mark 9.2–10, but with a significant difference. The basic outline is the same, but the version in Luke contains an additional central section of the transfiguration story, in vv. 31–2, and in particular the first of those two verses tells us what Jesus was talking about with Moses and Elijah. (As an aside, we are now engaged in the murky depths of redaction criticism, and it is only fair to note that of course we do not actually know what the three of them said, since presumably no one, not even Peter, overheard it, and Luke's account comes through some chain of interpretation perhaps from Jesus and/or Peter, and thus the precise words Luke uses are Luke's and not necessarily Jesus' or Peter's, but in fact this simply underlines that we are engaged here in the literary analysis of how Luke has told his story, rather than in simple historical reconstruction.)

Luke 9.31 tells us that they were speaking about Jesus' 'departure, which he was about to accomplish at Jerusalem'. The word for departure here is *exodos*, and while one cannot complain about the translation, what is lost is the resonance which this word has for the people of God, whose very identity was forged in the Exodus event, through the seawaters which opened before them and then closed over Pharaoh's army, as they went forward into their own promised land.

Where does Jesus stand as he contemplates the future of his ministry, already embroiled as he is in an Israel of conflicting messianic hopes, with religious authorities who are worried that his relaxed approach to some points of *torah* interpretation is just the kind of thing which is causing Israel trouble, and who is perhaps beginning to wonder what his calling might be in the light of this? Perhaps Jesus is looking at a traumatic ministry every bit as decisive as a new kind of exodus: a new leading of the way out of the old world and through trials to come (not a trial by sea, but certainly trials of some sort), followed by the glorious arrival in a new land as yet unimagined.

Could this new exodus involve a 'taking up' . . . ? And here we recall the word used in Luke 9.51 (*analēmpsis*), which we next encounter in Acts 1.2, where Luke casts a backwards glance into his Gospel to see Jesus being taken up to heaven. If we had but time and knowledge of the Greek translation of the Old Testament (known as the Septuagint, or LXX) we would find this same word used in 2 Kings 2.9 as Elijah turns to Elisha, his soon-to-be-promoted assistant, and asks what he can do for him 'before I am taken from you'. Finally, we recall that Elijah's extraordinary departure, between earth, sky and, somehow, strangely, death, saw him ride a whirlwind into heaven on a chariot and horses of fire: *taken up* into whatever it is that awaits us beyond this life.

Now we begin to see why Luke 19 was so reticent about trumpeting the moment of arrival: when Jesus arrives in Jerusalem it is a goal of sorts, but it is not his final destination. Jerusalem was to be the place where Jesus, having set his face to his mission, to the way ahead, would be taken up in order to fulfil that mission. The real goal of the journey is heaven. Luke 9.51 sets up an image of Jesus setting his face to return to heaven, by way of Jerusalem. It is perhaps not too much to claim that Luke 9.51 is the pivot, the turning-point, of Luke's entire Gospel.

Furthermore, we might note at this point that it is only in Matthew and Luke that we find genealogies of Jesus, tracing his line back through the generations to what turn out to be interesting starting-points. In Matthew chapter 1, that most extraordinary choice for a first chapter for the New Testament, the line goes back to Abraham, father of the Jewish faith, and telling us, if we have literarily-attuned eyes to see it, that Jesus' role within the scheme of Judaism is to be a major concern of Matthew's whole book. In Luke chapter 3, the line goes back further, to God, in a very unselfconscious reference back through Seth, then Adam and then God, as if Luke were really only saying what everyone knows. Why God, and why only here? Is it because Luke wants to say that Jesus comes from God, from heaven, which, whatever else it is, is always the abode of God, the place where God is. Jesus begins by coming from heaven, down to dwell among us through the nativity story, shepherds, embodied humanity and all, and begins his ministry, right up to the point where he sets his face to be taken up, to go to Jerusalem, yes, but to go beyond Jerusalem and return to the Father, to heaven. Luke's entire Gospel, perhaps, is one big *chiasm*, one big 'there-and-back' structure: and it turns around the central moment of 9.51.[2]

The other Gospels have similar moments. In John 12.23 'the hour has come', and there is a very similar sense of moving from an account of Jesus' ministry among humanity to the pursuit of his glorious return to heaven. In Matthew and Mark, the turning-point seems to gravitate more naturally around an incident recorded in Luke 9.18–20, the debate about Jesus' identity where Peter answers that Jesus is 'the Messiah of God' (in Matthew 16.13–20 and Mark 8.27–31). The effect is largely the same: a new sense of purpose and direction which turns Jesus' ministry towards its goal. Luke may have read Matthew and Mark of course, and got the idea from them, or at least if they were already available then they may be among the accounts he says he has considered in Luke 1.1. Either way, this shows that all of the Gospels, and not just Luke, have particular ways of telling their stories, and that at least sometimes we need to think of how a verse or saying or incident works in the wider context of the overall Gospel story if we are not to miss some important aspect of it.

An opposite way of putting the point is equally important. If we realize that some verses are basically doing the job of building up the bigger narrative, drawing out the bigger picture, then we will be freed from trying to find some kind of self-contained theological message in every detail of the biblical text. Some parts of it will be helping us on our way, putting us in touch with the wider journey that the text is inviting us to take, and enabling us to grasp that bigger picture. These texts will not make great sermon texts, but without them the sermon texts would lose their context, and in the end would lose some of the power which comes from seeing them in context.

In these three chapters we have only scratched at the surface of Luke's 'orderly account'. But the insights of the various passages we have considered invite us to read with opened eyes to see what is really going on in these all too familiar texts, our eyes opened by theological, historical and literary concerns. As I have endeavoured to show throughout these three chapters, it is the biblical text which invites us to take up these different hermeneutical approaches.

Having begun to explore the issues of biblical interpretation raised thus far, many people find themselves wondering, at about this point, how we can be sure that we are not imposing our own patterns on the text. The simple answer is that we can never be sure of this, although one proof of the hermeneutical pudding is in the eating, and if these approaches have succeeded in generating insight then they are to some extent justified by their practice. But in my judgement we *can* be sure that the questions we have been pursuing are at least put to us by the text.

More than this, to choose the alternative way of reading only on the surface without digging into the historical or literary issues relevant to interpretation is *not* the same as avoiding all hermeneutical judgements. Rather, it is to make a certain set of hermeneutical judgements, namely, the ones that suppose that we do not need any of this kind of information to interpret the biblical text.

At this point it is important to bring in the fact that many people would say they have theological reasons for doing just this. Those theological (and doctrinal) reasons, such as the much-maligned doctrine of the 'clarity of Scripture', or some particular view of biblical authority or inspiration, need to be assessed on their own terms, and it is to this task that we now turn.

♦ Part Two ♦

THINKING THEOLOGICALLY ABOUT SCRIPTURE

♦

♦ 4 ♦

The Difficulty and Clarity of Scripture: Of Problems in Romans

♦

Then what advantage has the Jew? Or what is the value of circumcision?

My guess is that most of us will not have thought about these questions much recently. If anything, we will not have thought about them at all, unless we ourselves are Jewish people, or have Jewish friends. And for many Christians, at least those who are not themselves Jewish, the most probable answer to this question is often 'I'm not sure – is there any advantage?'

These two questions make up Romans 3.1, and while we can quote Paul's answer with little difficulty ('Much, in every way'), many of us would not be able to explain it very easily, and most of us would be at a loss to know why he raises this matter at all. Romans has a lot to say about Israel, not least in chapters 9—11 which conclude with Paul saying, 'and so all Israel will be saved'. These are among the most debated chapters in the whole Bible, with the implications stretching as far as political and economic policies around the globe, all heavily invested in having a view one way or the other about the status of God's chosen people: the Jewish people.

I should say immediately that this chapter will fall a long way short of 'explaining' Romans, although along the way various suggestions about some of its interpretative puzzles will be made. Rather, my focus is on showing how the book of Romans raises significant questions of interpretation, as well as how it helps us to reflect on what is known as the doctrine of the 'clarity of Scripture'. Alongside this doctrine I would like to set the *difficulty* of Scripture, which is not, to my know-ledge, an equally well-known theological position, but which can certainly be maintained alongside a view of 'clarity'. These are modest aims, at least in comparison to the mighty book of Romans, but their effects are far reaching in turn in their own ways.

Let us start with the clarity of Scripture. In fact, let us start with Martin Luther. Luther's famous insight, at the heart of the Reformation, was that the God who alone is righteous is himself a justifying God, who shares his righteousness with others. As a result, the believer made righteous need have no fear that the righteous God will turn him or her away at the last day, but can be confident instead that they will be recognized as righteous, bearing indeed the righteousness of Christ.

The word 'righteous' has appeared several times in that brief explanation, and just as we saw with Luke 18 it is good to remember that 'righteousness' and 'justification' have the same Greek root, and that the verbs involved thus have very similar meanings, except that in English, unfortunately, we do not have a verb 'to righteous' which could be interchanged with the verb 'to justify'. As a result we need a whole lot more theological language to do the work of linking these two words, but this is not a major problem.

The real issue in the brief 'Reformation in a theological nutshell' presented above is the fear. The justified believer need not be afraid: no condemnation, in fact, for those who are in Christ Jesus, which is Paul speaking in Romans 8.1, as well as being Charles Wesley's great rallying cry in his hymn/ commentary on Romans, 'And Can It Be': 'No condemnation now I dread'. This was a real issue for the young Martin Luther, who was very afraid. Luther became a monk at the age of twenty-one, beating his body to pursue righteousness, to drive sin from his mortal flesh. What if he were inadequate to God's demands? What if he fell short of God's moral standards? What if the sin which crouched at his door mastered him? For Luther, who never did anything by halves, this was an obsessive quest for purity and perfection in the face of a literally awe-inspiring God, awe inspiring in the sense of terrifying. A righteous God, seen from this angle, and it was the pervasive angle of Luther's time, was a frightening prospect.

Luther's great insight hinged on his interpretation of Romans 1.16–17, a short statement which is worth laying out in full and then considering carefully:

> [16]For I am not ashamed of the gospel;
> it is the power of God
>   for salvation
>   to everyone who has faith,
>   to the Jew first
>   and also to the Greek.
> [17]For in it, the righteousness of God is revealed
>   from faith to faith;
>   as it is written, 'The one who is righteous will live by
>   faith' [Habakkuk 2.4].

But we have already gone too fast, for of course Paul did not write this in the NRSV translation, but in Greek, and if there is one book where this really makes a difference it is Romans. It is probably not an overstatement to say that if you only read the book of Romans in one English translation, no matter how good that translation is (and the NRSV is one of the best), you will never understand why the book of Romans has been so fiercely fought over down through the centuries. In this case, the phrase 'the righteousness of God' is the problem.

The little word 'of' is often a symbol of an ambiguity in the Greek text. There is no corresponding word in the Greek, which in the case of 'righteousness of God' reads *dikaiosunē theou*. These two words mean 'righteousness' and 'God', but how are they linked? The usual way in to understanding this translation issue is to consider the phrase 'love of God'. When we talk about the love of God, we could be discussing two quite different things:

1 the love which God has for us, as in 'the love of God is without limit', or

2 the love which we have for God, as in 'the love of God is sadly often submerged by the love of chocolate'.

In practice it is artificial to construct sentences like these which try to pin down one meaning only, and most of the time the two senses can coexist happily side by side, as in 'the love of Christ urges us on', which occurs in 2 Corinthians 5.14 with just such a potential double meaning (our love for Christ and Christ's love for us).

What then of the 'righteousness of God'? Luther's starting-point, since it was the evident truth of the matter, widely accepted by all, was that God was righteous, and hence the righteousness of God was a characteristic of God. This was precisely what worried him. How could a righteous God possibly accept sinful human beings? His flash of insight, his 'a-ha!' moment, was to see that *dikaiosunē theou* could refer to a righteousness that we have *from* God: thus something that God gives to us. As he turned this insight around in his mind Luther came to see that this shed a whole different light on the matter.

Luther lived at a time when Church practices, to simplify a hugely complex story, had occasionally strayed from the theological spirit of Paul the apostle. In particular it was common to buy 'indulgences' to earn time off purgatory, which was a bit like an immediate post-death waiting room before heaven, and, regardless of the merits of such a system, it was suffering from abuse and corruption at the time. Indeed the protest against indulgences was at the heart of Luther's famous ninety-five theses, nailed to the church door in Wittenberg in 1517. The last thing Luther had in mind in all this was the fragmenting of the Church into irreconcilable factions, but to his immense dismay that was the way the protesting movement began to go. The insight about indulgences encapsulated the fundamental problem of the (catholic, i.e. worldwide) Church of the time: the tendency towards what is known as 'works righteousness', which is the view that one could earn one's way to being righteous by the performance of certain works, including, though not limited to, the buying of indulgences.

Not all of Luther's theological insights were brilliant, as his understanding of the status of the Jewish people indicates with appalling clarity, but, in just the way that God seems interested in using such imperfect vessels for the achieving of his purposes (King David, anybody?) so God used Luther's insight about righteousness to achieve a radical reorientation of Church thinking, a reorientation traditionally, although somewhat problematically, labelled 'the Reformation'. (As so often, the label tells us more about the labellers than about the issue.)

It is perhaps inevitable that a discussion of Romans includes consideration of Luther's views. The point is this: in reacting against medieval Catholicism, Luther saw how the book of Romans spoke in a very different theological voice from that of the Church around him. The leap of understanding which follows this insight is the following, fallacious one: if Luther (inadvertently) created Protestantism out of reacting against Catholicism, then Paul, fourteen centuries earlier, must have been basically arguing about what Luther was arguing about, and therefore early Christianity was essentially reacting against a form of Jewish works-righteousness. This gives rise to the typically Protestant reading of the New Testament, and especially Romans, as a book about justification by faith, in contrast to an old covenant which must, we assume, have been about justification by works. On this view, Christianity offers freedom from a Jewish legalism which today's reader assumes was a lot like medieval Catholicism.

This is a powerful and widely held theological reading. It is almost certainly mistaken as a summary of what Paul thought he was saying, although in its affirmation of grace against works it captures a basic theological insight. Where it goes wrong is in building a picture of Judaism as a religion of works simply to be a foil for the new word of grace. In our chapter on the Pharisee of Luke 18 we began to see that this is far from the truth, at least as far as our historical understanding goes. So why is it that so many people have seen Luther's view as self-evidently doing justice to Paul? To answer this we need to take a detour through the question of why Paul wrote Romans in the first place.

The book of Romans is a letter like any New Testament letter. In other words it is a document written in a particular context for a particular reason. This normally urges caution on just how far we should go with deducing theological propositions from a letter, but in the case of Romans does not seem to do so. Some say this is because Romans does not really have a context: it is a kind of last attempt by Paul to write down something which could be called his 'gospel'. Perhaps there is something in this, although more likely it has a very specific context, tied up with the commendation of Phoebe in 16.1–2, the sister who is the deacon of the church in Cenchreae. She is described as a *prostatis*, or financial benefactor, perhaps the one who funded Paul's work, and perhaps the one bringing Romans as an advance letter from the apostle who hopes to visit soon. (The NIV keeps its head down at this point by saying that she has been 'a great help', but this is a very weak translation.)

Paul's imminent visit is of great relevance to our understanding of Romans. In chapter 1.10–13 he explains how he has long intended to visit Rome, but now at last plans to do so. In chapter 15 he clarifies why, since he has now finished his work in all the regions from Jerusalem round to Illyricum, which is roughly the area of Albania and the former Yugoslavia. In v. 24 he tells us that he is on his way to Spain, not for a spot of well-deserved sunbathing, but to strike out, apostolically, into new areas. In short: he has evangelized the whole of the East and is now heading West. And what should lie en route but Rome? A chance at last to visit, and perhaps to get some financial support for his mission. In the words of one commentator: Romans is 'Paul's letter of recommendation *for Paul*'.[1] Incidentally, Paul's statement that 'there is no more place for me' in v. 23 is a bit of typical Pauline exaggeration, or else it is a rueful reflection on all the places he has been thrown out of. Probably the former.

The key question now is how Rome will receive him. Paul and Rome do not perhaps see eye to eye on everything. Rome was apparently the home of Peter, traditionally the first pope, which is doubtless anachronistic but retains the insight that Peter was based in Rome. And Paul and Peter had a stormy relationship. 2 Peter 3.15 seems to speak through gritted teeth of 'our beloved brother Paul' whose letters are hard to understand. In Galatians, which is Paul's angry young man letter, his confrontation with Peter and the various other 'pillars' of the Jerusalem church, probably back in the 40s, was plain for all to see (in 2.11–14). Romans is written in about AD 57. What is the issue which is likely to be causing trouble?

The issue is not a simple one. It concerns the status of Gentiles as members of the people of God. More pointedly: God had clearly promised in his written word that his people, called out *from* the nations to be a blessing *for* the nations, would have a king to reign over them eternally, a land in which to dwell forever, and would belong to God forever. These promises were clearly about the Jewish people. Now the people responding to the gospel included significant numbers of Gentiles, that is, non-Jews. Yes, this was obviously good news in its way, but where did it leave those promises to God's people? Fundamentally, if Gentiles could now be part of the covenant without following *torah*, didn't that mean that *God had changed his mind*? And in terms of Paul coming to Rome, we must remember that Peter, the leader among the first apostles, was the pillar of the early Church: the rock who provided leadership to God's people in the first days after Pentecost. Paul was the apostle to the Gentiles. We may have every reason to conclude that Rome is basically suspicious about what gospel Paul is preaching, since it seems to be weak on *torah* observance, and it apparently allows Gentiles into the covenant in the place of God's own people. We can summarize all this by saying that Romans is indeed a contextual letter, like every New Testament letter, but the context includes: 'what is Paul's gospel?' If Paul is going to get Rome's support for his journey West, he needs to explain just what it is that he preaches, and indeed what he believes.

Now we come to the crux of the matter. Paul could have conducted a very simple argument: in the past God gave the Law, but now we are saved by grace. That was then (and it was the Old way, the Old covenant, the Old testament . . .). This is now (the New way, the New covenant, the New testament . . .). That was by following Moses, and obeying the Law. This is by following Jesus, and receiving the gift of justification. This is a fairly simple argument, but it is not Paul's argument in Romans.

The main reason Paul does not argue this way is because it would suggest that, somehow, what had happened before was not God's own perfect work, and this is something which Paul cannot accept. In the words of Romans 9.6: 'it is not as though

60

the word of God had failed'. In the two preceding verses Paul has listed all that Israel was given: adoption, glory, covenants, and at the end of the list, possibly, the clearest New Testament reference to the divinity of Jesus: the Messiah, who is God over all. (This reference, in Romans 9.5, is difficult because we do not know where to put the comma in the punctuation, i.e., whether it should read 'the Messiah, God over all be blessed' or 'the Messiah, who is God over all, be blessed'. There is no obvious right answer to this question.)

Romans chapter 7, with its doing and not doing which serves as such a tongue-twister for many an unwary public reader of Scripture, is also wrestling with this issue: 'if I do what I do not want, I agree that the law is good' (v. 16). This is exactly *not* what the average Protestant reader of the passage expects to find, but it is what Paul feels he must say since otherwise he will cast doubt on the perfection of *torah*, and any imperfection there would reflect badly on the God who gave *torah* in the first place.

Hence, to begin to complete the circle, what advantage is there in being a Jew? Much, in every way. And, although Romans 11 remains always a debatable passage, it certainly seems to affirm something about how the salvation of Gentiles provokes Jewish people to turn to the living God, the God of Abraham, Isaac and Jacob, now revealed to be the God of our Lord Jesus Christ. Therefore there is now no condemnation (8.1), but what is often breezed over straight after this verse is that 'God has done what the law, weakened by the flesh, could not do' (v. 3), and the weakness of the law, of *torah*, comes not from any imperfection within it, for as we have seen this would be unthinkable to Paul, but from sin which somehow got inside the law. Deep in the twists and turns of Romans 7 comes the link between law and sin that seems to clinch this line of interpretation: 'the law is holy' (v. 12) and 'it was sin' (v. 13). This is a strange kind of separation of the law into its holy and corrupted natures, which then in turn is matched by the strange separation in every person between their slavery to the law of God and to the law of sin (v. 25). Who will rescue us from this body of death, that is, this fractured and split self, pulled inexorably both ways (v. 24)? The answer, as always: Jesus, offering us wholeness instead of this brokenness. It is heartening to realize, immersed as we are in the intricacies of the most theologically profound text of the New Testament, that the old Sunday School dictum is right once more. The answer is Jesus, and for those who are *in Christ Jesus* (8.1) there is now no condemnation.

Now back to where we came in, at 1.16–17. Paul is not ashamed of the gospel, which we notice is 'to the Jew first and also to the Greek'. Now we see why this is part of this basic manifesto-like statement for the whole letter. God's righteousness was dispensed freely to the Jews, and now to the Gentiles also. It moves *from faith to faith* (v. 17). A review of different translations demonstrates conclusively that we do not really know what this means either. Literally it reads 'out of faith to faith'. Perhaps it is a way of underlining the centrality of faith in the Christian life. Perhaps it is something to do with the faith of Jesus.

The faith of Jesus is another topic tied up with one of the 'of' problems in Romans. To highlight the issue here we start with the NIV, which seems to find Romans on the whole a very uncomfortable text, needing a great deal of decisive translation to make sure the gospel comes across clearly. Recall that the key 'Lutheran' understanding of the gospel involves the gracious reception of the gift of righteousness. Romans 3.22, NIV style, offers something of a proof-text here: 'this righteousness from God comes through faith in Jesus Christ to all who believe'. But a theological problem lurks within this approach: if the unearnable gift of salvation is to be so strongly contrasted with the 'good works' approach of the other side (whether or not they are medieval Catholics) then what exactly qualifies us to say that we have put our faith in Jesus Christ? Is this not the most decisive 'work' of all? Faced with this problem, it is usually argued that this work is actually the work of God, who supervises it somehow along with the work of the individual. Perhaps this is so, although it is hard to see how one could really know this. But our question is simply whether the verse was saying this in the first place.

The phrase translated 'faith in Jesus' here is *pisteōs 'Iēsou*, 'the faith of Jesus', and once again it can be taken in more than one way: the faith we put in Jesus, or the faith which Jesus has. In this case the issue is compounded by the fact that *pistis* can be translated not just as 'faith' but also as 'faithfulness'. Perhaps the key idea is that the righteousness *of* God (not just 'from God' as in the NIV) is secured by the believer through the faithfulness of Jesus. In other words, because Jesus was faithful in his calling and mission to the point of obedience to death, God's righteousness is now available for all (both Jew and Gentile). If Jesus had not been faithful, the righteousness would not have been secured for us. In case this sounds as if it is arguing that righteousness was not in any case available through the *torah*, we note that 3.21 sets us up to be talking about a righteousness 'apart from the law', a new revelation, yes, but not a new concept of grace, since grace was there in the old way too.

Translation issues go along causing trouble all the way through the book of Romans. 'The obedience of faith' (1.5) is perhaps faith, described as obedience, or perhaps it is obedience, brought about by faith. 'The offering of the Gentiles' (15.16) could be a collection, *the* collection in fact, mentioned in 1 Corinthians 16 and collected by Paul to attempt to impress Jerusalem with the generosity of the Gentiles, coming to the aid of the famine-struck city and thereby showing the Jewish people that the Gentiles were on their side (a very

Romans-sounding argument). Or perhaps it is simply the Gentiles themselves.

And in Romans 5:12, in a phrase consisting of no more than three letters in Greek, *eph ho* (the *h*s don't count in the letter count), Paul appears to say that all sinned because one sinned. What he actually says is so brief that it is hard to pin down: death came through one man . . . and so death came to all, *eph ho* all sinned. Straightforward ways of taking the words might include 'upon whom' or 'because of which', but what does that mean? Most modern translations take it along the lines of 'on account of', and thus argue that Paul is saying that death came to all 'because all sinned' (or 'in that all sinned'). But if we took a different line of thought we would end up with the traditional idea of all sinning 'in Adam': 'upon whom' read (probably unhelpfully) as 'in whom'. In doing precisely this, many traditional interpretations have found a statement of how 'original sin' works: the male seed passes down in genetic continuity and in this strangely mythical 'literal' sense we were 'literally' in Adam, all that is except the one who was not born of a man, Jesus himself, preserved free of the stain of original sin. Thus Augustine, lining up the passage with a view of sexuality as fundamentally stained by sin. But perhaps the three letters don't add up to that interpretation at all, and mean to imply only that, since all have in fact sinned, all are subject to death.

Romans is a difficult book. It breaks into glorious clarity in places, where the argument happens to coincide with some-thing already believed, but it consistently refuses to fit into theological frameworks brought ready-made to the text. The truth that God reaches out graciously to all, both Jew and Gentile, seems evident throughout. This much is clear. How that works, and how it can be that what is new is good with-out downgrading what was old, that seems destined to remain obscure.

In reality, Paul is arguing in a very tight corner: the old way was God's, and it was good, but the new way is better, although that doesn't mean that the old way was worse, and it will all work out in the end. We want to ask how. We want to ask, especially, where today's Jewish people stand with respect to the righteousness of God, and it seems clear that Paul himself sees this as a question which his argument inevitably raises, which is why he tackles it in chapters 9—11. But when it comes to the crunch, and he wants to say 'and so all Israel will be saved' (11.26) he manages to leave it as a 'mystery'. In which, I suspect, we would be wise to follow him.

Luther's fear was driven away by the power of Romans, by its removal of condemnation and its offer of unconditional righteousness through grace and faith. It was several centuries before Krister Stendahl, in a brief little article on this whole issue, wondered just how far Paul had the same kind of internal angst that Luther had. In 1963 he wrote about 'the apostle Paul and the introspective conscience of the West'.[2] Paul, he pointed out, was not wracked with guilt, not even in Philippians 3, where, for the sake of knowing Christ Jesus, he is willing to count all his great zealous achievements as worthless, or as 'rubbish' (or in fact as *skubalon*, which is a swear word for excrement, whatever the translations may say). Even then, it was not that Paul was troubled, or guilty, or desperately looking for what he did not yet have, since in fact he was already a zealous servant of the God of Abraham, Isaac and Jacob, and this was *the right God*. That much he would maintain until his dying day (some time shortly after 2 Timothy, in all likelihood). Rather, somewhere along the Damascus Road, he discovered that serving this God meant following Jesus instead of persecuting him, a 'conversion' in some senses to be sure, but not a switch of gods.

What then shall we say? The clarity of Scripture did not extend to the point where it was all clear, this much is . . . clear.

The clarity of Scripture was designed to safeguard the insight that Scripture is *clear enough*. It is available to all. It offers enough guidance to allow us to live. It tells us that the answer is Jesus, and it even seems to suggest that this is the right answer to a whole variety of questions, but it does not necessarily even guarantee that we will be able to see how this works, as with the resort to 'mystery' in Romans 11.25. If we unleash the doctrine of the clarity of Scripture from these carefully defined moorings, and try to turn it into the claim that all things in Scripture should be understandable by everyone, then we actually move away from the traditional Christian view of the matter. Romans itself is further indication that Scripture is happy to remain difficult in many, many ways, without compromising the clarity of the gospel, even if the same could not be said of certain translations. Stendahl hits the nail on the head when he writes, with a wonderful economy of expression:

> Lutheran tradition just knows that the purpose of Romans is to teach justification by faith without the works of the law. Calvinists just know that it is the chief text from which to get the proper doctrine of predestination, and Catholic tradition takes the second chapter as its chief text for substantiating its glorious and correct doctrine of natural law. Augustine, by mistranslating, found the doctrine of original sin in chapter five.[3]

And he is right. We all just know that the way we see it is the way it is, but we do not all see it the same way (the ecumenical problem in words of one syllable).

Scripture is clear, let us say, on the macro level. On the micro level it is persistently difficult to pin down. With respect to Romans, it works a bit like this. Paul was assuming that everyone already knew that Judaism was a religion of a covenant and the covenant was established by grace. The covenant was for the people of God, generally seen more as a group than a collection of individuals, which is a largely modern way of thinking. *Torah* was the framework given to allow God's people to stay within the covenant. Keeping *torah* did not earn the right to be part of the people of God. Put this way, this is exactly the issue a Christian faces today when they wonder whether they are doing what the Bible says in order to be a Christian, or because they are a Christian. The Christian probably wants to say that it is the latter even though sometimes it feels like the former. Paul perhaps would have said the same. Be that as it may, Paul's point is that this basic way of understanding the life that God wants is comparable for both Jew and Gentile because of the way that God's righteousness has now been revealed in Jesus.

Now if you read Romans in a situation where the basic framework is not in place, such as Luther's position in the sixteenth century, what strikes you is less that the framework applies both for the Jew and Gentile, which is not really your issue, but that the framework is what it is in itself, namely justification graciously given by a righteous God. The particular version of the framework which strikes you, as a Christian, is the half which shows how this has now been revealed in Christ. The other half, frankly, seems like a series of 'Old Testament illustrations' or 'sidetracks' or, as some see Romans 9—11, digressions on the topic of predestination. That the continuous argument of Romans does not fit neatly within this view is the foremost internal clue that Romans was not originally addressing this agenda, but it is important to realize that we can still see that it has something to say, indeed something very powerful to say, to this agenda. Which is why Protestants who come to Romans and hear the gospel of justification preached from it cannot really understand why anyone would be anything other than a Protestant, and NIV readers, most likely, cannot see how one could take Romans seriously and not be an evangelical Protestant. In Stendahl's terms: we all just know that we are right.

The other aim of this chapter, more in passing than directly discussed, was to try to underline the difficulty of Scripture. There is no obvious theological reason why every believer should be able to read Scripture for themselves and work it all out: this is an individualistic vision which seems likely to be at odds with the way Christian wisdom works. It is certainly fair to say that any Christian who can read can attempt the task of understanding the biblical text, but to read a translation, as we have seen, is already to hand over quite a bit of theological judgement to others on the perfectly fair grounds that they have a technical competence which the beginner does not have, and which most Christians will never develop, modern life being what it is.

In Part One of the book we looked at three types of context for reading the Bible: theological, historical and literary. In a sense, this chapter has added a fourth: the linguistic context. The New Testament is first a Greek text, and a particular kind of ancient Greek text at that. It is true that for many purposes, and in many cases, we can read the New Testament in English translation without worrying unduly that perhaps we are missing the main point. As we have seen, however, we do inevitably miss some things. But it is mistaken to say, as some do at this point, that all that the Reformation achieved was the introduction of a new priesthood, the 'priesthood of the scholarly expert'. Clearly most of us are ill equipped to judge the latest scholarly findings on what a particular Greek phrase meant in a particular context, but there is a freedom for discussion, scholarly accountability and the tests of time and reflection which makes most scholarly suggestions a good deal more negotiable than the views of a priest might have been in a preliterate and largely immobile rural congregation.

Scripture is difficult. But it is sufficiently clear for getting on with life. As Luther might himself have said.

♦ 5 ♦

The Inspiration and Canon of Scripture:
The Breath of God
and the Rule of Faith

2 Timothy 3.16

♦

No book on the Bible would be complete without consideration of 2 Timothy 3.16, one of the many '3.16' verses which
seem to invite being appropriated out of context as banner-
waving theological statements, whether it be John 3.16 at a
football match, 1 John 3.16 ('We know love by this, that he
laid down his life for us . . . '), the curse of the woman in
Genesis 3.16, or the little-known Leviticus 3.16: 'All fat is the
Lord's', that great promise for the overweight.

2 Timothy 3.16 will tell us that all Scripture is inspired. It
will not tell us what that means but, with a bit of theological
and historical reflection, we will discover quite a few things it
does not mean. We will also end up looking at the 'canon' of
Scripture, a term which will need careful definition. All of this
will go towards building up a picture of the Bible as God's
book, and thus hopefully go some way towards meeting the
objection that hermeneutics is unnecessary since the real issue
in biblical interpretation is to hear God's voice today, regardless of what the historical human authors thought they were
doing. My claim: it is not one or the other but both.

Here is the verse, from the NRSV translation:

All Scripture is *theopneustos*
    and   useful
        for teaching,
        for reproof,
        for correction,
        and for training in righteousness.

The structure of the verse seems clear. Two things are said about Scripture: that it is *theopneustos* and useful. Let us take, for one moment, the meaning of *theopneustos* as 'inspired' and come back to it presently. What Scripture is useful for is also clear: four different activities, although generally when people make a list of four activities they are seldom saying 'four and only these four' but rather giving an account of the kinds of things Scripture is useful for. Nevertheless all the listed uses gravitate around the idea of instruction in Christian living.

Owing to a certain flexibility in Greek word order, there is actually a possible ambiguity in the phrase 'all Scripture', which could mean either that 'all Scripture is inspired' or it could mean that 'all inspired Scripture is ... '. Clearly the latter option could suggest that only those parts of Scripture which are inspired are useful, opening up the possibility that only selected parts of Scripture are inspired. Most translations do not take this path, and the reasons are not grammatical but conceptual. It is of course possible that Paul was saying that only the inspired parts of Scripture are useful, but on the whole this would have been quite a claim, since it was generally assumed that Scripture, which at this time was what we would call the Old Testament, was inspired, whatever that word meant at the time. The argument therefore runs that if Paul had wanted to make a case for partial inspiration then it would have required more than a passing reference. This is evidently not a conclusive argument but, as we shall see in this chapter more than once, conclusive arguments are not exactly in abundance when it comes to a doctrine of inspiration. We shall therefore stick with the traditional rendering of the verse, as quoted above.

What really matters is what *theopneustos* meant. The word can in this instance be broken down into its component parts: *theos*, meaning God, and *pneustos*, breathed (rather like the *pneuma*, the spirit or breath). Words cannot always be treated this way, as is obvious from trying to analyse 'butterfly' into butter that flies, but in this case it can be done. Which leaves us with 'God breathed' as a good translation for 2 Timothy 3.16: all Scripture is God breathed. The traditional interpretation is thus 'inspired', which does have a technical sense of 'breathed into', but misses out the fact that it is God who is doing the breathing. It also raises the interesting question of whether God is breathing *into* Scripture or more *out* of it, that is, through it, and it has been suggested that we could call Scripture 'ex-spired' by God in order to capture precisely the nuance of meaning.

Two other points are worth exploring here. First, we need to ask about the context of this verse. It is all very well to quote it as a free-standing point about the inspiration of Scripture, but why did Paul say it? Was he engaged in the task of setting up just such a doctrine? No he was not, and in fact the context of the verse in 2 Timothy 3.10–17 demonstrates that Paul's concern is to encourage Timothy in the godly lifestyle which he has been pursuing, fitting in with the notion that this is a sort of farewell letter from the one to the other. Timothy is exhorted to 'continue in what you have learned and firmly believed', reminded that one of the resources for just such a continuation is the Scriptures that he has known since childhood. The context is that Timothy is to continue to let his life be shaped and moulded by the Scriptures he has already been working with, knowing then that these Scriptures come with the imprint of the very breath of God. The goal (v. 17) is that Timothy might be equipped for every good work.

This is as practical a context as one could wish to find for reflecting on the use of Scripture, and it touches on the nature of Scripture only in the clarity with which it makes its practical point. Paul does not define what he means by 'inspiration' if it is to have some semi-technical sense, and so it seems best to work with the passage on its own terms and leave it at the level of 'God breathed for practical purposes (i.e. teaching, training in righteousness, etc.)'.

The second point follows on from this, but takes us further into the question of how to build our doctrine of Scripture. It is sometimes said that the 'inspiration' of Scripture is a characteristic of only the 'original manuscripts': in other words the texts as they were originally written down, but not as they were copied. Here we need to know something of the mechanism by which the biblical text has been passed on from its original writing through to its preservation in later Hebrew and Greek copies, and then on into translation. When Paul wrote a letter, and if it was thought worthy of wider circulation, for example, among the various churches of the time, it would be copied out for this purpose. Inevitably, over time, variations would creep in between different copies. In so far as we have a variety of ancient versions of any biblical book, this is still a relevant point today when an edition of the Bible has to choose between alternative copies, or 'readings', as they are known.

The discipline devoted to this issue is 'textual criticism', and the various possibilities for some verses occupy the footnotes of different Bibles. To give a simple illustration: the verb in Philippians 2.10 has two different spellings in different texts, representing two different 'aspects' (close to what we mean by tenses). In one case it is saying 'that every knee will bow' and in the other 'that every knee could (or might) bow', with the one reading suggesting that all will one day voluntarily worship God, while in the other the bowing may be a forced acknowledgement. This particular case does not usually merit a footnote, but it ties in a quotation of Isaiah 45.23, the question of whether Philippians 2 contains a 'hymn' which Paul is quoting, and a point of theology about the final state of all people before God. In the previous chapter we saw how this kind of question navigates between the difficulty and clarity of Scripture. Here the question is different: which of these two readings is 'inspired'?

This question, or at least questions like it, is widely asked along the more conservative end of the theological spectrum, but it reflects a modern tendency across the whole range of theological views to seek the earliest possible meaning of a text as in some sense definitive: whether of what the author intended, or what the text meant, or means. The tendency is to pursue the earliest text as the one that God wanted, with later alterations reflecting deviations or corruptions away from the pure norm. This view of life is something of a modern phenomenon, and it is ill equipped to deal with the biblical text which we actually have.

There are perhaps biblical books where there was one definitive author's version of the complete work. Philemon might be a good candidate for this status. But more often there is not any necessity to imagine one fixed first text, and with a book such as Acts, for instance, there are at least two major versions of the text in circulation (known as the 'Western' and 'Eastern' texts). On the whole these issues do not threaten the mainstream of theological tradition, and in any case that would be to take the discussion off in a different direction, but what they really do is undermine the whole approach of saying that a characteristic of 'biblical inspiration' can be said to apply to some 'original manuscript' in a way in which it does not apply to later copies of the text.

We should go further. In 2 Timothy 3, the Scriptures which are described as *theopneustos* are the ones Timothy has known and been using since his childhood. These would primarily be the Scriptures of the Old Testament, but in fact they would be the Greek translation of the Old Testament, the Septuagint. Thus in so far as 2 Timothy 3.16 bears on any doctrine of inspiration, it actually opposes the idea that biblical inspiration could apply to the original manuscripts, and requires instead that it apply to the version of the Scriptures accepted into use by the Church. From the modern perspective, with its penchant for accuracy and originality, this appears to be an ominous retreat into a subjective mess, but we must accept that this is not the way it looked for most of Church history, and that rather it transfers the weight of the argument about the inspiration of Scripture to the community which takes Scripture seriously. (There *are* problems here too: basically we replace one set of issues about the biblical text with another set, about the nature of the Church, but these seem more likely to be the questions we would need to address.)

The discussion so far has circled around 2 Timothy 3.16 with enough of a view of its context to allow us to begin to formulate a doctrine of the inspiration of Scripture. Other biblical verses clearly relate to this topic, and we should briefly consider three of them. In 2 Peter 1 we find the claim that 'no prophecy of Scripture is a matter of one's own interpretation, because no prophecy ever came by human will, but men moved by the Holy Spirit spoke from God' (vv. 20–1). Here is a clear indication of 'inspiration': what the men said was derived somehow from what God wanted to say. If anything, this idea is probably more commonly in mind when people talk of the inspiration of the Bible than the ideas of 2 Timothy 3.16, but we need to note that the precise manner of how this 'speaking from God' works is not given in this passage, and also that the whole claim only relates to prophecy, for which it seems eminently suitable, while it is more problematic to see how it could relate to wisdom literature, or a psalm of complaint, or a genealogy, for example.

John 10.35 has Jesus saying 'the Scripture cannot be broken' (NIV) (or 'annulled' – NRSV) and this seems to offer some clue about the guaranteed success of Scripture's goals or intended effects. This claim is best made by skating rather quickly over the unusual context, which finds Jesus arguing with 'the Jews', who in John's Gospel, we have to assume, are not Jewish people in general, but some particular section of the Jewish people, perhaps those in Jerusalem, who are the targets of some of the most vicious characterization in the entire Bible (e.g. 8.44).[1] These Jews are accusing Jesus of blasphemy since he has just said 'the Father and I are one': what clearer indication could they need of the fact that Jesus sees himself as equal in some sense with God? Jesus' response is that their own law says 'you are gods', speaking of those to whom the word of God came, in Psalm 82.6. This psalm sets God in his rightful place as ruler of the divine council, a picture well known in the time of the psalms, and in the surrounding nations, but one that might be a little problematic to us today if we were to take it as a real description of how we see God's role in the universe. Nevertheless, it is this psalm which prompts Jesus to say that 'the Scripture cannot be broken'. Does Jesus really believe that Psalm 82 is a depiction of the way the world is? What seems more likely is that he is conducting an argument against those Jews who are accusing him, pointing out that by their own lights the Scripture cannot be broken. Thus, argues Jesus, they themselves are ill placed to accuse him of exactly what Psalm 82 says is true of anyone to whom the word of God came. Perhaps John thought this was a good argument, which is why it turns up in his Gospel, but perhaps he is just recording the incident. Either way, John 10.35 offers little evidence that Scripture's divine origin ensures that it is incapable of failing in its aim (a view which is usually labelled as the 'infallibility' of Scripture).

A third relevant verse would be Matthew 5.18, from the

Sermon on the Mount, which has Jesus say, 'Until heaven and earth pass away, not one letter, not one stroke of a letter, will pass from the law until all is accomplished'. When this did or will happen, and what it implies for the ongoing status of the law (the *torah*) is no simple matter to determine, as indeed the whole Sermon on the Mount in Matthew 5—7, for all its black and white ethical appeal, turns out to be one of the most complex sections of the New Testament to interpret. All I can do here is recommend a good book, and wonder if one day I might even understand it myself.[2]

Inspiration: a biblical text filled with the spirit, or breath, of God. Something to do with the idea that the Bible we have is the one that God was happy to leave with us, copying errors, grammatical problems, historical and ethical hard questions notwithstanding. The desire of some to turn the Bible into the book that they would have produced had they been in God's shoes, whether the 'they' in question is on the left or the right of the theological spectrum, needs to be resisted, and seen for the dangerous form of spiritual pride which it often is. This is not the place for a discussion of all the different theories of inspiration, such as 'dictation' or 'accommodation' which all attempt to pin down the answer to the question, 'How do the words of the biblical text relate to the word of God?'[3] In my view, these discussions usually need a more thorough look at what exactly we (and the Bible itself) mean by 'Word of God', and this would take us into a whole new area (which we shall touch on in the final chapter below). Instead, I want to consider the related question of the 'canon' of biblical books that we now have, and see how this adds further light to our discussion of biblical inspiration.

It is an obvious point that if you held in your hands a copy of, say, 1 Corinthians, removed from its context as a 'New Testament book', you would not by looking at it be able to deduce that it was more than a letter. It would clearly look like what it is: Paul's letter to Corinth. It might stand out to you because it is theologically profound, or because you are a female prophet and a bit concerned about its contents. But it does not have a footnote: 'inspired bit of the Bible'. This raises the historical question so easily passed over by a lot of simplistic theories of inspiration: how did the early Church recognize an inspired document when it saw one? Interestingly enough, not even the most conservative of early Church theologians ever seriously put forward the idea that God was inspiring the selection of books in the same way that God inspired the books themselves. So how did we end up with this particular collection of Bible books and not another? For the sake of simplicity I shall focus here only on the New Testament.

The 'canon' of Scripture is not just the list of what is in it, as if 'canon' were a piece of theological jargon for 'contents page'. *kanōn* was the Greek word for a reed, or a reed used as a measuring rod, and thus a 'straight rod'. From this it developed the sense of a norm or a standard, and it is used in this way in Galatians 6.16: 'as for those who follow this *rule* (*kanōn*) . . . ' (and also in some variant readings of Philippians 3.16, thus a delightful combination of another '3.16' verse with the issue of textual variation). By the late second century, the particular norm or standard which matters is *ho kanōn tēs pisteōs*: the canon (or rule) of faith, more commonly known by its Latin name, the *regula fidei*. This rule of faith is the 'norm' or 'standard' by which the Church measures whether something has authority for its faith and life: in other words, this is its canon. The 'rule of faith' was never defined in an official set of words, such as the creeds were, but appears to have been loosely derived from Romans 12.3, where Paul urges that we think of ourselves appropriately, 'according to the measure of faith' which God has given us. 'Measure' here is *metron*, from which we get the ideas of metric, metre and so forth, but the idea is the same as saying that there is a norm or standard of faith. In so far as this is found in writings, then, the Church comes to say that its 'canon' is its collection of writings. Thus by the middle of the fourth century, the 'canon' exists both as a list of writings and as an authoritative measure built into those writings.

It is important to get this argument right historically. Many factors went into the adoption of a text as part of this canon, and the canon has an inbuilt theological 'standard' which ensures that what is in it is useful for faith and life. Some of the factors involved were whether a book was written by or derived from an apostle (e.g. Mark's Gospel was said to be developed from the apostle Peter's recollections), whether a document had relevance beyond its original setting (so that Paul's letters had something to say to a wider audience than just the original intended audience), whether a document was theologically orthodox, had some kind of track record in being used constructively in Christian living and worship, and whether it was deemed 'inspired' by God. The key here is to recognize that these factors cannot all be separated out and analysed one by one, but that they work together and demonstrate over time that a book plays an ongoing role in the Christian faith.

This 'vagueness' about exactly whether a book measures up to the 'canon' standard or not should suggest that there would have been some debate about whether a book did or did not measure up, and in fact this is what we do find if we investigate this issue. The question of whether 2 Peter or Jude should be included went on for ages, and as late as the Reformation prominent leaders were lamenting the fact that Revelation ever got in and whether it was really too late to do something about it. In the third and fourth centuries there was considerable variation concerning the later books in the New Testament as to whether they were in or not. It is worth pointing out that the Gospels and major Pauline letters were hardly ever at stake, and this gives us a fairly solid and mainstream grasp of just what the theological standard is (or was) by which these other books were judged. The book of Jude appears to have got in because it was written by Jude, the brother of Jesus. That it quotes a lot of non-scriptural sources in the course of its short and relatively unspectacular argument caused some concern, and appears to be why pretty much the entire argument of Jude reappears in 2 Peter 2, with all the non-scriptural references removed. I am still waiting to meet someone for whom the inclusion of the book of Jude has made a key difference in their Christian life, although a few years ago I did develop a Bible study and a sermon on the book, for that most worthy of spiritual motives, to show that I knew something about a really obscure bit of the Bible.

The evidence also demonstrates that quite a few books which in the end did not make it in to the canon were included at various times and places, such as *1 Clement* (an epistle) or an apocalyptic work entitled *The Shepherd of Hermas*. A knowledge of these books is of great help in understanding early Christianity, and in the process can shed a lot of light on New Testament texts. It is also often the case that there is little that is exceptionable in these books: to read *1 Clement* is to find some fairly familiar exhortations to faithfulness and rebuking of splits and quarrels, issues which we find in the New Testament letters too.

This whole issue is not only a matter of historical interest. The discovery in 1945–6 of what is now known as *The Gospel of Thomas* at Nag Hammadi in Egypt, as part of a large 'gnostic' library of texts dating back to the second century, raised the whole question again. (Gnosticism was an approach to faith which emphasized secret knowledge, 'gnosis', and it is hinted at in various places in the New Testament, but it only fully developed in the second century.) Should *Thomas* be included in the New Testament? Is it, as some scholars have argued, a fifth gospel, and thus to be published alongside the other four, as the 'Jesus Seminar' in the United States has done?[4] How could we tell?

The Gospel of Thomas is a short collection of 114 numbered sayings ranging from some which we also find in the Gospels through to sayings which fall some way short of the tests of orthodoxy or 'traditional usage'. Just the last two sayings illustrate this very well: Thomas 113 is basically Luke 17.20-1 (Jesus responds to a question about when the kingdom will come by saying that even while people say 'look here!' or 'look there!' it will not come that way, but it is spread out on the earth and people do not see it). In Thomas 114, however, Jesus responds to a comment that women are unworthy of 'the Life' by saying that 'every woman who makes herself male will enter the Kingdom of Heaven'. End of gospel. Hmmm. Overall, then: close but no cigar. *The Gospel of Thomas* is fascinating reading, but falls *theologically* short of the 'canon', the standard of the rule of faith which has always been the unofficial heart of Christianity against which all statements, documents, letters and gospels are measured.

What we find, therefore, is that built in to the very concept of 'the Bible', or for our purposes 'the New Testament', there is already a theological framework. It comes from the life, the teachings, the deeds, the death and the resurrection of Jesus, and when written documents come along which encourage constructively the task of reflection on, and the living out of, this story, they are admitted into the New Testament. *This* is in fact what we were after with our pursuit of the doctrine of inspiration: a way of understanding Scripture as useful for the tasks of Christian living. Yes, this is a circular process, but it is inevitably circular, and not viciously so (perhaps again it is a spiralling process).

It is a process hidden away in the name 'New Testament' itself: which comes from the Latin phrase for 'new covenant' (as used in 1 Corinthians 11.25 and 2 Corinthians 3.6), and which has the basic ambiguity as to whether it means that these Scriptures *are* the new testament/covenant, or whether they are *about* the new testament/covenant. Either way this observation brings us back to a view of inspired Scripture which sees it as providing us with access to the central story of Jesus and all he did and accomplished, understood according to the rule of faith, or the 'measure' of faith with which God has measured out understanding to us.

The process of continually checking and clarifying what that means in terms of the ongoing voice of God today, through biblical interpretation and hermeneutical discussion, is the ongoing work of the Church in all its many different contexts around the world, and onward into the future. For such a wide-ranging and endlessly flexible task, the kind of looseness which we have discovered in a 'biblical' doctrine of inspiration is entirely appropriate, and the emphasis it places on the Church's developing of faithful and wise interpreters of Scripture is also appropriate.

It is sad that all too often discussions of 'biblical inspiration' are divisive and overtechnical. Let us leave the last word to Karl Barth, who with typical passion moves beyond the technicalities (though he is not afraid of them), and reminds us 'Finally, as regards the doctrine of inspiration, it is not enough to believe in it; one must ask oneself: Am I expecting it? Will God speak to me in this Scripture?'[5]

◆ 6 ◆

The Authority and Application of Scripture: Learning to Live with the Bible

◆

I was sitting in a panel discussion on biblical interpretation, which is not something I do often, but which had happened as a response to an interesting sermon on the book of Nehemiah. The sermon had argued that much of the book of Nehemiah, which concerns the rebuilding of Jerusalem after the exile, does not apply today. In particular, we are not expecting the rebuilding of the temple in modern-day Jerusalem: these kinds of issues have been taken up by the way that Christ in the New Testament fulfils all these various hopes and expectations of the Jewish people.

The panel discussion was throwing backwards and forwards the question of whether the book of Nehemiah applies or not, and then which bits of it apply, and why and when, and I was there because I was supposed to know something about hermeneutics, although I didn't particularly know much about the book of Nehemiah. I had not managed to say anything helpful, at least as far as I could see, and I was getting more and more confused by the various arguments about whether this or that bit of Scripture applied to us, when suddenly an idea struck me: the problem was not in the issue of what the book of Nehemiah was about, but the problem was with what we meant by the world 'applied'. I opened my mouth: 'I don't think the Bible applies at all,' I began, but I did not get much further, because this idea was perceived by all concerned as so far off the map as not to be worth taking seriously. But I have become convinced that the idea is worth taking seriously, and so although I would no longer put the point in the same way, in this chapter I shall basically defend the view that we are usually muddled when we talk about 'applying the Bible', and that there are better ways of saying what we want to say.

I think something similar can be said about notions of biblical authority too, and indeed authority and application seem to be two sides of the same coin. In the end, the Bible is not fundamentally about principles to be applied, or about authoritative rules to be obeyed. (I will want to say, of course, that it is about Jesus, or at least nearly so, but we will come to that presently.) And the book of Nehemiah, in any case, is thin on principles and rules, which is why it is a particularly bad candidate for 'applying to us'. Nehemiah is a story and, in a different sort of way, so is the whole Bible. To live with the Bible is to live with a story. This chapter is basically a consideration of what that means for the questions of biblical authority and 'applying the Bible'.

The phrases 'biblical authority' or 'authority of the Bible' are so familiar that we tend not to think much about what they could possibly mean. What kind of authority would we want to say that the Bible has? Perhaps it has moral or ethical authority. To say that the Bible has this kind of authority would suggest that in moral and ethical matters what the Bible says is right. No object-carrying on the Sabbath, then.

Interestingly, many people who take this line end up with the kind of morality which reflects quite well on their own way of living: the Bible turns out to be in favour of an honest hard day's work for those putting in the honest hard days, but it is in favour of the poor if you ask the poor what it is about. Whether the Bible really has one consistent moral opinion about smoking, or drinking, or dancing, or swearing, or tax returns, or fair trade coffee, or any of the other key social issues in the rural and small-town world of two or three thousand years ago is another matter. (It doesn't always have a consistent opinion on lying, for that matter.)

Perhaps the Bible's authority is 'religious' or 'theological'. In other words, what it says about how to live the religious life, or what it says about God, is authoritative, even when all those sayings are couched in strange and far-off cultural ways. This kind of approach works well too if you keep your distance from the text, and end up with the God of introductory school classes in Religious Studies (RS). My very first RS lesson at school left a strong impression. We had to memorize the meanings of three words about God: omniscient, omnipresent and eternal. It was only many years later that it occurred to me that the first two of these words do not feature much in the Bible. (We also had to memorize Isaiah 55.8–9, and I do not know which version this was, but I memorized 'My thoughts, says the Lord, are not like yours, and my ways are different from yours, for as high as the heavens are above the earth so high are my ways and thoughts above yours', and this is close to the NRSV when I look it up, although I memorized it more as one long polysyllabic word 'mythoughtssaysthelordarenot-likeyoursand . . . ', which interestingly enough we recall is closer to the way the ancient manuscripts of the Bible were written. I think Isaiah 55.8–9 was chosen to cover the teacher in case we ever felt that RS lessons made no sense.)

It is a matter of some disbelief to people such as myself, brought up with this kind of philosopher's god, to actually read the Bible and find that it talks of a God who repents. It does this in the flood story (Genesis 6.6–7), and in 1 Samuel 15.11, where the word of the Lord comes to Samuel and says, 'I regret that I made Saul king'. Samuel obviously had the same RS teacher as I did, because he cannot quite believe it either, and takes the first chance he has to harangue King Saul by saying, 'The Lord has torn the kingdom of Israel from you this very day, and . . . will not recant or change his mind; for he is not a mortal, that he should change his mind' (vv. 28–9). This is yet another example where paying close attention to the text of the Bible is a quick way of dispensing with a lot of theories about what the Bible must surely say.

Other kinds of authority could be added to our list. Some say the Bible has 'salvific' (or 'soteriological') authority: in other words, it is authoritative on the matter of 'how to be saved'. Others, mainly in more recent times, insist it has factual authority, a status as a dispenser of scientific truths which leaves it tangled up in all the well-known arguments about six-day creation, dinosaurs, the sun standing still, evolution and who Adam and Eve's children married, which should really be enough to warn off anyone from going down this fossil-strewn path. Perhaps the Bible has authority about matters of philosophy or general knowledge, such as what truth is, or a kind of psychological authority, correctly dividing the human self into its three constituent parts of spirit, soul and body in 1 Thessalonians 5.23, although this seems no more assured than that the bowels are the location of compassion, as the Hebrew idiom has it frequently through the Old Testament (thus Jeremiah 31.20, 'my heart yearns for him; I have great compassion', in the NIV, though it literally begins 'my bowels rumble').

What this survey of unlikely ways of pinning down biblical authority shows us is that we really need to backtrack and ask a more fundamental question in the first place, which is why we want to talk about biblical authority at all.

There are two classic answers to this question. The first focuses on what the Bible is: its *nature*. It is, say defenders of this approach, true, it is inspired (although this is often left hanging as a vague threat rather than being given the kind of substance we looked at in the last chapter), and it is the Word of God. These are facts about it and they are such powerful facts that they simply do result in it being authoritative.

A second approach looks at what the Bible does: its *function*, and hence it is sometimes called (usually a bit dismissively) *functionalist*. What does the Bible do? It reveals God to us, it inspires us, it transforms us. These things could be done in a whole variety of ways: a beautiful sunset might inspire us, and might even reveal God to us in some way. *1 Clement* might reveal God to us, to recall our discussion in the previous chapter. Defenders of the first view tend to see this second view as a little too subjective. Each side has a good go at showing why the other is inadequate: how can the truth and inspiration of the Bible suffice if we do not pay attention to how to interpret it and the effect it has on us? How can the Bible reveal God to us in reliable ways if it is not inspired, true and so on?

More recent attempts to break through this argument attempt two different approaches to the question of authority. The first is to say that both sides of the dispute had fair points. What we actually need are the insights of both positions, because the *function* of the Bible is intimately tied up with its *nature*, and you cannot have one without the other. What the Bible is in itself is not really the issue (how could an unread book really be authoritative?) but what the Bible does depends on what the Bible is. To take an example, the promises of the Bible can be effective only if certain things are true about them. If the end of Matthew's Gospel sees Jesus promise that he will always be with his disciples, then it is one thing to see this as an encouragement or, loosely, an inspiration, but for it to work as a promise it has to be true that the one saying this is really Jesus, who is capable of being present in this way, in some 'real' sense. Likewise, it is because the Bible is 'breathed out' by God that what it says about God can be revelatory: that is, is more than just Paul's or Isaiah's impressions. In other words, the function of the biblical text depends on some true things about it. This approach falls under the heading of the study of 'speech acts', which is an approach to language which points out that words achieve effects depending on who says them and in what context. On the whole it is a very promising way forward for thinking about how the nature and function of the Bible are linked.

A second way ahead which has gained ground in recent years is the view that 'authority' is one useful image for talking about the Bible, but it is not the only one. There are in fact many images we could use of the Bible to suggest ways in which it still speaks today, and 'authoritatively' is one of them, but only one. Thus David Clines offers the intriguing possibility that the language of authority derives from male-dominated ways of thinking about how to influence and be heard:

> Strange in a way that feminists have not yet seen that 'authority' is a concept from the male world of power-relations, and that a more inclusive human language of influence, encouragement and inspiration would be more acceptable to everyone and more likely to win the assent of minds as well as hearts.[1]

He does not mean 'inspiration' here in the sense of 'inspired Scripture', but in the general sense of seeing how the Bible inspires us. This view tends towards being a bit weak on specifics, but it does have the merit of taking seriously the complexity of hermeneutical thinking which clouds the way from the text to the reader. How does the book of Nehemiah inspire or influence us? This is a good question which in principle is answerable, rather unlike the problematic 'How does Nehemiah apply to us?'

The question of what other images could be used to describe how the Bible speaks today leads us directly into the question of 'application'. If the Bible were simply a historical document, of antiquarian interest only, it is doubtful that we would be overly troubled by its frequently odd details and assumptions, of the kind that we have been examining throughout. But the biblical text still speaks today for as long as people listen to it, and indeed it even speaks in odd ways when people do not really listen to it but just happen across it out of context and poorly understood. In extreme cases it even speaks when it is attributed with saying things it simply never says, like my friend who kept her house clean because, she was sure, the Bible said that cleanliness was next to godliness.

Walter Brueggemann offers the delightful image, not intended irreverently he assures us, of the Bible as a 'compost pile': a place where new texts, once written down, are thrown on to the pile of the old ones, and as they bed down and take up residence in the canon so they grow and mutate in unpredictable ways to create whole new ways of looking at things.[2] The Bible as compost pile is a particularly striking off-beat metaphor for the concept of the living word today, but it is admittedly right down one (unusual) end of the spectrum. The discussion of biblical authority more usually broadens out into asking just what we mean when we say that 'the Bible applies to us today'.

The language of applying the Bible basically seeks to bridge the gap between the Bible and us somehow. The question is: how? Does it ask, 'What biblical principles arise out of the passage?' This I think is the most common way of thinking, and it has one very serious drawback: it assumes that whatever the kind of text we have, what we are *really* looking for is principles, and if we do not see them in the text then we need to find them by drawing them out of the text. The kind of principles involved are then typically the moral and ethical ones we considered earlier. For some biblical texts this can work. In general it tends to force all biblical texts into this moral and ethical framework.

We can try to simplify the question and ask, 'What does the Bible say today?' One well-known series of devotional commentaries bears just such a title: 'the Bible speaks today'. This is fair enough, but in itself does not constitute an answer to *how* it speaks today. On a personal level, many Bible readers want to ask, 'What does the Bible say on a personal and immediately relevant level to me?' Again this leaves us guessing about how we can evaluate different 'applications' of the Bible. A friend of mine used to enjoy appealing to the story of Samson in the book of Judges whenever the conversation turned to the vexed matter of God's 'guidance' in daily life. Samson sees a Philistine woman at Timnah in Judges 14.1 and after his parents try hard to dissuade him from marrying out of his own people, he resolves the discussion with the forthright appeal 'Get her for me, because she pleases me' (v. 3). His father and mother, says the story as it continues on its untroubled way, 'did not know that this was from the Lord' (v. 4). Here, my friend would say, was one of God's ways of guidance: holy lust.

A more promising way ahead, and there have been hints of it through not just this chapter but the whole second part of the book, is to say that the question of application is best understood as saying, 'What does a biblical passage *reveal* to me about . . . ?' whatever we are asking about, perhaps about God, or Christ, or creation. The key point here is that the Bible says much about many things, many more in fact than it ever intended to discuss, and that does mean that a lot more is pulled into the 'biblical' orbit than anyone ever intended, but what the Bible does specifically which sets it apart from other literature is that it *reveals* God to us. What we have arrived at is the argument that we need a doctrine of revelation in order to read the Bible wisely.

What then does the Bible reveal? Of course some might say that it reveals a lot of facts or truths, but this underestimates the force of the argument about 'the rule of faith' in the previous chapter. The inbuilt theological standard which we saw at work there suggested that the revelation of the Bible centres around Jesus, his life and death, his teaching and deeds, and most of all his resurrection, without which the whole of Christianity is a great programme for moral living and looking after our neighbours, but it lacks the central ingredient which makes it Christianity. Recall that we argued back in Chapter 1 that we must read the Scriptures in the light of Jesus and understand Jesus in the light of the Scriptures. There too I allowed that this way of putting the matter needed to be broadened out to take in the doctrine of the Trinity rather than just saying that it's all about Jesus. Here too we need to take the broader view: as theologians would say at this point, the Bible is God's trinitarian self-revelation. In fact, this is exactly what Karl Barth said in his powerful article on 'The Strange New World within the Bible'.[3] We read this extraordinary story of Abraham, of Moses, of the prophets, of Jesus, of the early Church, and what do we make of it? Is it an account of history? Yes, in a way, but such an odd and selective one that this cannot have been the point. Is it a book of morality? 'Large parts of the Bible,' says Barth, 'are almost useless to the school in its moral curriculum',[4] a point not lost on any good moral parent who has read the Bible to their children and stumbled over the stories of death to Sabbath wood-carriers, incest and rape in and out of Israel, or the matter of 'holy lust' which we considered above. Barth is equally scathing of the notion that we find 'religion' in the Bible: not if we define religion as the ways in which people organize their lives and thoughts in pursuit of God. No, what we find in the Bible is God reaching down to God's people everywhere, throughout history and onward to the present day: the revelation of God, who is Father, Son and Holy Spirit. More specifically, we find the story which is told in order for God to reveal that this is his particular trinitarian identity.

Barth's argument has not really been bettered. The emphasis

91

on the Bible as God's *story* has become very prominent in recent years. This is partly because it appeals to the more story-orientated leanings of what some people call this 'post-modern' world (a label which seems to mean a huge variety of things, some helpful and some not). But it is partly because it really does seem to do more justice to the nature of the Bible to describe it as a story than as a work of doctrine or even (narrowly understood) as 'systematic theology'.

N. T. Wright invites us to imagine Scripture along the lines of a five-act Shakespeare play, where the biblical text takes us through the first few acts, leaving us, as the Church today, to improvise the final act while remaining 'in character'.[5] We work within the possibilities of those first acts: creation, fall, Israel, Christ, the Church . . . This is our story, as God's people, and we 'implement' it today. Not only is this a creative and persuasive account of biblical authority, as it sets out to be, but it actually offers a very good answer to the question of what it means to 'apply the Bible' today, and it gets us away from the constant problem in the contemporary Church of reducing the Bible to the level of morality by finding everywhere within it moral principles for us to apply, as if the gospel were the good news that we all get to try harder than ever to be good moral people. Which of the Pharisee and the toll collector knew how to 'apply' the Bible? And which received the gospel?

The language of Moule may reflect a way of putting the point which dates it slightly, but the theology is just right: 'The Bible is not itself so much a compass or a chart, as directions for finding the Pilot; and he it is who will be to us both compass and chart and will steer us through.'[6] In fact, one could also say that Shakespeare's five-act plays are not exactly common currency these days either. Let me close this chapter, then, with an attempt to sketch out this whole approach to Scripture's authority and application with an example drawn from more recent times.

I will never forget the dramatic experience of watching the first *Star Wars* film when it first came out in the cinemas in Britain in the late 1970s. As an impressionable young boy in the pre-video and pre-computer age, the film totally caught my imagination. In particular, the spectacular concluding scene of the Rebel X-wing attack on the Death Star included a shot of the entry of the small spaceships swinging down into the Death Star trenches for their final approach. I sat glued to my seat as the picture on the enormous screen in the cinema lurched one way and then the other to simulate the twisting flight down into the depths. You could feel the reality of the moment, as real as any car ride, plane flight or bike ride down a dark alley. To emerge, blinking, into the sunlight of a quiet London suburb a few minutes later was to leave the world of *Star Wars* and re-enter my normal world, but as a changed person, for I was now someone who had survived a flight to the Death Star and back.

On the whole I am delighted with the advance in technology which now allows me to watch this self-same film on video on the tiny TV screen we have in our living room. But the moment of approach to the Death Star is never the same, for there in the small corner of the room, surrounded by bookshelves, pictures, toys, the noise of cars outside and footballs flying over the fence, the twisting camera work does not make me lurch in my seat at all. It is all too small scale, and does not overcome my world, and neither can I fully enter its world.

Apart from the obvious 'application' that I should buy a bigger television, what is the point? Recently I was preaching on Acts 16.16–34, the story of Paul and Silas in prison in Philippi. Since I had studied the passage through the week, I arrived on Sunday morning quite impressed by it, but the rest of the congregation arrived on Sunday morning not having the faintest idea that this would be the set passage, and instead fairly preoccupied with other things, the typical ups and downs of any week of living in our complicated and tiring world. The passage was read, as Scripture is always read as part of the service, and then I walked up to preach. I realized, as I listened to the reading and looked around the church, that for almost everyone this passage was playing on a small-screen television. It was probably a television in the kitchen, and they had one eye on not burning the lunch and one eye on the story of Acts 16. There goes the slave girl, there go her owners, there go Paul and Silas into prison, there they are singing hymns, and then – look at that! – there's an earthquake. They get out, the jailer believes, everyone gets baptized, and then it's time to put the potatoes on and check the dessert.

This small-screen viewing of the story is, I think, typical of the way most of us are exposed to Scripture most of the time. And it leaves us (or it left me at that moment) pondering just what sort of 'application' one could make from this Acts 16 passage. I duly informed the congregation that if ever they were in prison in first-century Philippi for exorcising the demon of a slave girl, and there was an earthquake during a time of midnight hymn-singing, then this passage would apply perfectly to them and show them exactly what to do.

This met with some surprise and a fair amount of scepticism, but it made for a lively sermon. In fact, I tried then to suggest that the only way to hear a word from God from this passage was to stop playing it on our kitchen-corner television set, and watch it on the big screen of the cinema, gripped by the earthquake just as I had once been by *Star Wars*. Watch it this way and then, when you emerge blinking from church half an hour later, you might be changed by what you have seen. In this case, you might be changed by the extraordinary God who was at work in that passage, a God who will pin you to your seat if you stop and watch, but whose hand you might not even notice on the mini-TV version.

The 'application' of the story comes through the wholesale

effect of being transformed by watching/hearing it properly, as a word about who this God is that we are trying to know and love in our Christian lives. To meet with God in the story is to be changed. There is no guarantee that God will shake the foundations of any prison you might ever end up in, and I knew that this would be a false word of spurious hope to bring from a passage such as this. But there is a guarantee that the God who is revealed in this passage is the same one we live with today, and that guarantee comes from accepting that this Scripture is 'inspired', built to match the 'rule of faith', and thus authoritative in this strange new way that we have been looking at in this chapter.

If this is what we mean by saying that the Bible 'applies' to us then so be it. For myself I tend to think that it is not what we mean, and so I prefer to say that the Bible does not apply. But either way, if it wakes people up, and makes them take God seriously, then that is what matters.

♦ Part Three ♦

REVELATION

♦

Unveiled Eyes and Unveiled Text

♦

The book of Revelation is the place where it all comes together: theologically, historically, literarily, imaginatively and hermeneutically. This chapter offers a way in to reading Revelation which tries to bring together the various insights of earlier chapters. To many, this will sound like trying to explain the difficult by appealing to the impossible.

Revelation is the happy hunting ground of religious lunatics and extremists, or of people whose great concern in life is how premillennial you are, and, for most of the rest of us, it is a hunting ground that is closed to the public for the foreseeable future, awaiting development at the end of the world, veiled from our understanding. But this is to miss out on one of the most remarkable and (though you may not yet believe this) one of the most immediately relevant books of the entire Bible. In particular, we concluded the last chapter by saying that the Bible is fundamentally about God's self-revelation. In the book of Revelation, the veil which so often hides God from our eyes is drawn back. And what do we see when that happens? If we play it out on the cinema-sized screen, rather than the kitchen TV, I think we see something like this.

We see John, on the island of Patmos (1.9). We are, then, looking at a historical text, and we might want to know that Patmos is a Greek island, and John might be in prison, perhaps because he was publicly testifying to Jesus. The only thing we probably do know about the book is that he is going to write seven letters to the different churches in the region, which will get us as far as the end of chapter 3. Then a door will open in heaven, there will be lots of choruses and hymns, worship of the lamb on the throne, and then after that it will all gradually get weird, wild and either worrisome or wonderful, depending on where we stand.

The letters to the seven churches, which are really several sections of one letter sent to all seven churches, so that each one gets to hear what is good and bad about all the others, is usually the only section of the book preached or studied in most churches today, although I did once turn up at a Bible study group where I was visiting to be told that 'we are up to Revelation 16, looking at the sixth and seventh bowls, and discussing where Armageddon will be', which was as strange a welcome as I have ever had anywhere.

I will be brief with the seven letters, therefore, except to note that the reason why there are seven of them is because seven was a number of completeness in the early Church, and thus in the Bible, and it recurs frequently through the book. We may also note that the function of these seven letters seems to be that these seven churches represent, in some sense, the whole Church: some are good and some are in a mess, and each faces different trials and possible blessings. We can almost always relate our own position to one of them, and so we are reminded that the book of Revelation will speak to our kind of situation too. I am not sure we could ever 'apply' it though.

This is not a one-chapter 'commentary' on Revelation, but we do want to see how an awareness of different contexts for the book can help our reading. First, what sort of literature is it? It is known as 'apocalyptic', a word which has increasingly come into popular usage through the medium of films such as *Apocalypse Now*, with its dramatic images of the American helicopter assault on an unsuspecting Vietcong village against the soundtrack of Wagner's 'Ride of the Valkyries', one of the most unforgettable sequences in modern cinema, in its own wide-screen and appalling way. That kind of 'apocalyptic' imagery is what many people see in the book of Revelation too, and in one notorious case the locusts from the bottomless pit in 9.7–11 which are described as having wings like the noise of many battle chariots and tails that sting like scorpions have been described as prophecies of modern-day helicopters, which we shall shortly see is a rather overliteral way of approaching the text.

In fact 'apocalypse' is simply the Greek word for 'revelation', and either word means 'unveiling'. Apocalyptic literature was common at the time, although this is the only booklength version of it in the New Testament. The most important thing to understand about it, in terms of its theology and its historical classification as apocalyptic literature, is that apocalyptic is *not about the end of the world*. At least, not in the sense that we might think. What it is actually about is *revealing*, and in this case what it reveals is God, the God of Jesus Christ and of the Holy Spirit, who is the Lord even over the chaotic world of the end of the first century, where John has been thrown in prison and all seems lost for a church facing persecution (and we do not need to decide the tricky question of whether there ever was an actual persecution in AD 95–6, the traditional date of the book, since it is enough to know that it was threatened). When God is revealed as he is in the book of Revelation, something does end, but it is not the world. It is the way we see the world. Our whole outlook on the world is changed by this unveiling, and we begin to see the world around us in ways we had not seen it before. And so I would suggest that Revelation is a book about *the end of the world as we know it*, in the sense that it changes the way we know, and changes what we know, about the world in which we live.

The unveiling begins at the point where most churches leave the book, at the beginning of chapter 4: 'After this I looked, and there in heaven a door stood open!' (4.1). How many doors are there in heaven and how far do we have to look to see them, or see past them? Well, according to John 14, Jesus said that in his Father's house there were many mansions (or dwelling places, as modern translations put it) and perhaps there are enough doors for everyone to have their own room? I doubt it. The opening door in heaven symbolizes the revealing to John of this God-centred reality in heaven.

What does John see? How he wrote it all down we shall never know, but the key thing which he sees is Jesus seated on the throne, Jesus as a lamb (5.6) even though he has just been described as the Lion of Judah (5.5), which is a significant contrast between an image of power and strength and an image of sacrifice and suffering represented by the cross. What is the lamb holding? He is holding a scroll (5.1) and nobody can open it. This scroll is key to the whole book.[1]

There is a very simple reason why no one can open the scroll: it is sealed. No one is worthy to open the seals, of which there are seven, which should not surprise us. The scroll is what will contain *the* revelation of the book of Revelation, and so one good question to ask is how it is opened and when. As we scroll down quickly through chapters 6—10 we discover that the opening of the seals is a significant activity, and that out of the first four of them come the infamous 'four horsemen of the apocalypse' (6.1–8). Each seal clearly seems to be standing for some event or observation about the world we live in, or more precisely the world which John's first readers lived in (or John's first hearers, since the book was designed for oral performance, according to 1.3, which perhaps still today offers a blessing to anyone who reads the book aloud).

The seals are interrupted after six out of seven of them are opened, and the interruption is also a sealing, of the 144,000, who seem to represent the people of God understood as a kind of standing army, ready to fight the forces of evil (which might explain the striking verse at 14.4 about the fact that they have 'not defiled themselves with women', since those preparing for combat were not to engage in sexual activity, a view developed out of considering Leviticus 15.16 alongside the passages which required holiness of warriors). The point here, however, is simply this: the scroll is still not opened, because the seventh seal is not opened until 8.1, and as soon as it is opened there is a sequence of seven trumpets being blown by the angels. These angels are from the throne room scene back in chapters 4—5, and so we are still watching the scroll being unrolled at this point. The trumpets, like the seals, symbolize the terrible events going on upon the earth, and they take us up to the appearance of 'another mighty angel' in 10.1. What does this angel have in its hand? A little scroll, not sealed, but open. In 10.6, the angel says, 'There will be no more delay'.

The key thing is to realize that the entire story up to this point has been the preparation for the revelation, the contents of the scroll. Now John receives the scroll from the angel's hand, and in 10.9 is told to eat it, which he then does. Here we have the 'seer', the author of this apocalyptic book, eating the scroll which contains the message which is to be unveiled, and then in v. 11 being told, 'You must prophesy again about many people and nations and languages and kings'. The idea of eating a scroll from God is found in Ezekiel 2.8—3.11. Ezekiel is probably one of the few candidates for being an even more obscure book than Revelation, but in this short section the point is clear: Ezekiel eats the scroll and thus 'inwardly digests' (somewhat literally) the message which God wants him to proclaim. So too here with John in Revelation. For Ezekiel the scroll was as sweet as honey, as it was for John, but in John's case it left a nasty aftertaste. John's message will be one of bitter judgement as much as of hope.

Thus we arrive at chapter 11 as the long-awaited contents of the scroll, and what should immediately strike the reader is that as soon as chapter 11 begins we are totally and completely lost in the middle of some very obscure (and unexplained) symbolism. This is perhaps a further indication that it is only now that we have reached the actual 'revelation'. Before proceeding to it, it is only fair to acknowledge that there are of course many different interpretations of Revelation, and not all of them see these two scrolls in chapters 5 and 10 as the same. The second one is indeed called a 'little scroll' whereas the first one is just a scroll. But with Revelation, it is the clarity of the big picture which counts in interpretation, and the difficulty of all the details needs to be measured against the overall understanding of the story. In this particular case it does not make a huge difference whether the two scrolls are the same, but it does matter that 'the revelation' itself only begins in chapter 11, which allows us to see the first half of the book as preparation for its main message.

The reader will have to look elsewhere for help with the details beyond chapter 11, but in many ways chapter 11 itself is the key, since it seems to be a kind of summary of the contents of the scroll, which is repeated and developed in subsequent chapters. In any case, chapter 11 is so full of strange details that it will keep us busy enough. The risk is that we will lose the overall focus if we get lost in the details.

To take one example: what are we to make of the 42 months and the 1260 days (11.2–3)? A little bit of elementary mathematics will tell us that these are basically the three and a half years which concerned Daniel in Daniel 7.25 and 12.7, and it will take us that long to read all the different theories about what that means, but essentially it is a way of referring to a time of great persecution, apparently described in months from the point of view of evil, but in days from the point of view of the faithful witnesses. We could recall that Daniel too was written at a time when God's people were under such attack that even their continued existence seemed in doubt. Revelation often draws on details of Old Testament symbolism in this way. Take the olive trees and lampstands in 11.4, which remind us of Zechariah. At least, to be honest, that is what all the commentaries say, although truth be told we have probably never read Zechariah, or at least never really understood it. Lampstands, however, featured in Revelation 1.20, where they were interpreted for us: a lampstand is a church. Why? Is it because it is a source of light for the surrounding people? Again, while the specifics may be difficult, the big picture can still be built up, and it is this which we will aim for as we read Revelation 11.

The two witnesses in 11.3, who play a key role in the chapter, are two in number because in the Old Testament (e.g., Deuteronomy 17.6; 19.15) you needed two witnesses to have a testimony which was considered valid. Chapter 11 describes these two witnesses in terms of Moses and Elijah, turning the water to blood as Moses did in the plagues in Egypt in the book of Exodus, and shutting up the skies so that there was no rain, as Elijah did in the book of Kings. We last saw Moses and Elijah on the Mount of Transfiguration, where Jesus was preparing for his *exodos* ('departure') in Jerusalem. But they are not named here, and this is because these two witnesses are not simply Moses and Elijah, but are also the whole Church, seen as faithful witnesses to Jesus.

Is this faithful witness successful? The overall message of the book is 'Yes!' This chapter tells us: No! And then Yes! Yes and No. How does this work? Is the Church to be successful in its witness to Jesus? If we can answer this question then we can begin to see what the book of Revelation is trying to show us, or reveal to us.

In 11.7 the beast kills the witnesses and they are left dead in the street. We do not yet know this beast, we have not been introduced, but when we are in chapter 13 we will not forget it quickly. Where is this street? It is Sodom. No, it is Egypt (the land of slavery before the Exodus). No, it is Jerusalem, site

105

of the crucifixion. Does John not know? Not at all: he is saying that the Church's witness seems to fall, to fail, in any place where evil seems to win, and as his list of cities suggests, this seems to happen a lot. New York. London. Bombay. Berlin. Mexico City. Wherever humankind gathers itself together to create cities, from the great city of Babel on through Babylon, Rome and up until today, God seems to be pushed out to the margins of the city.

The city, in the Bible, is humanity 'writ large', notoriously self-sufficient, and turned away from its creator God, for who needs a creator God when everyone can see that the city is a creation of the humans who live there. It is a tower that reaches up to the heavens and suggests that everything we have achieved we did ourselves, with good planning, clever resource management, exploitation of the planet's non-renewable resources, and the discreet deployment of cheap labour bussed in from the outskirts, or from the farthest reaches of empire, wherever that may be.

What do we see when we look at the city? We see the failure of the Church's witness, mirroring the failure of its Lord, who after throwing himself at Jerusalem, all those years and centuries ago, was left to hang on a cross and die, not even offered the dignity of a private death away from evil eyes. In 11.9, this death is even left on the streets, and in v. 10 the world rubs it in our faces, celebrating and exchanging presents. Let's build the biggest celebration of them all. Let's call it Christmas, and turn it into an event which celebrates the success of our man-made economies, and then let's disallow 'religious' elements for fear of offending anybody, and let's exchange the costliest presents we can find, perhaps some Nike trainers, perhaps made by a thirteen-year-old girl in a sweat-shop in a shanty town in the Far East who is paid not enough to feed herself or allow any in her family to escape from the relentless cycle of poverty and depression.

We look at the world around us and it is a mess. It is going to hell in a handcart. And meeting up once a week in small groups to sing 'Bind us together' turns out to have made about as much difference as Lot did in Sodom. That's it. That's the bottom line.

Until v. 11. The third day. (Or three and a half days in this case, rather like 'on the third day' at the tomb was really only thirty-six hours later, and the number is stretched here to match up to Daniel's 'three and a half', because something is about to happen which will so affect the nature of our reality that even two and two will not make four any more, but will add up to three and a half . . .)

After three and a half days, the breath (or 'spirit', *pneuma*) of life whips into the dead bodies, of the two witnesses, of the Church, and raises them to their feet. This is resurrection, which again was foreshadowed in Ezekiel, when the valley of dry bones came alive. The imagery here shifts easily between the third day, the day of Jesus' own resurrection, and the resurrected witness of the Church. Verse 12 sees the ascension to heaven. The enemies are terrified. Cue earthquakes: the shaking of the foundations of the city, any city, shaken down to its roots, as the witness to Jesus turns out, after all, to be triumphant.

How did that happen? Where does this resurrection life come from? This is the deeper reality which for most of us, most of the time, is veiled behind the deceptive way it seems to be. The witness of the Church to Jesus turns out to be a deeper reality in our world than the marginalization of that witness in the modern world, whether it is in the city, in the press, or in the secularization and extraordinary greed of Christmas. By the power of that breath of life, we did make a difference. And we recall that even Lot, who looked so much like a dismal failure when we read Genesis, was described in 2 Peter 2.7 as a righteous man, rescued by God out of his great distress at all that was happening in Sodom all around him.

Is that the way we see the world? Is this revelation an end to a way of seeing the world – the end of the world as we know it? This would seem to be the point. When the beast gets its full introduction in chapter 13 it is so clearly Rome, the empire which nobody would ever have believed would pass away, but which is now a chapter in the history books. The whole world loved Rome: the *pax romana* was the great gift of peace which made progress and development possible. If Rome offered to run things for you, you signed up and paid taxes, and reaped the benefits. You would have had to be as stubborn as a Pharisee to say otherwise. But Revelation says: don't look at Rome that way. Think of it as a harlot, a prostitute, a whore, clothed in great jewels and wondrous clothes, but actually the foulest and worst of them all (17.1–6). Rome is Babylon. Rome is Oxford Street. Rome is the West today. Does the reality of our Western world smell sweet to us, or is it awaiting unveiling, guilty of all that is said of Rome in the extraordinary lament of Revelation 18: the fall of Babylon, or rather the collapse of the empire, wherever and whenever that happens?

The only time I ever visited Berlin was May 1989. Six months later the wall was down: reality was upside down. The way the world had seemed to be had been unveiled: revealed as something we had not imagined, even if deep down we had thought that God would not be mocked by these man-made walls, both real and imagined (emotional, psychological, spiritual). In the West it was too easy to jump to the conclusion that here godless communism was receiving its just deserts, and God's own capitalism was being vindicated. The first time I preached on Revelation I said that this was surely not right, and that one day we would see capitalism unveiled in the same way. Three months later two planes were flown into the World Trade Center twin towers in New York, and we all watched amazed, weeping and wailing over the smoke of their burning as it seemed to rise forever, with that impossible realization that without justifying in any sense the acts of those who took life that day God would not be mocked either by the building of a capitalist tower right up to the heavens. An unveiling. A new way of seeing, for those with the eyes to see.

In the book of Revelation, the veil which separates God's way of seeing reality from our own usual ways of seeing is drawn back: the door in heaven is opened (4.1), and then the temple in heaven is opened (11.19), and finally heaven itself is opened (19.11) and Jesus rides out victoriously on the white horse. This triumphant ride is the last appearance of the Word of God in Scripture, as living and active as ever (Hebrews 4.12–13, where nothing is veiled from the Word of God), and completing in final recreating victory the creative work begun by the Word of God in Genesis 1, where everything was spoken into existence by God (which was really the point, rather than the six days).

As the rest of the book goes on to recount, the aim of all of this was that people from all nations would gather around the throne in the end: that every tribe and people and language would stand before the throne. The resurrection of Jesus becomes the resurrected witness of God's faithful people, so that in spite of the fact that everything in the world around us pushes Christianity out to the edges and suggests that it is a primitive superstition that we are now finally leaving behind, it turns out that God is still the one in charge of world history, and of all nations and empires, and is still engaged in the infinitely loving process of drawing all people to himself, and of bringing everything together in Christ (themes found in Ephesians 1.10 and Colossians 1.15–20, where the language may not be apocalyptic, but the scope of the vision is the same).

This 'victory' that has now been won by the lamb, what is it? It is many things, but I am delighted to report that the Greek word for victory is *nikē*, and that therefore, when God has done with this present world order, and brought us all at last into his new creation, his new heaven and new earth, his new Jerusalem, back around the tree of life which we were expelled from so long ago in the garden, that then we will be able to see the reality that is currently veiled from our sight: that *nikē* belongs to the lamb.

It is true that we cannot remain, on a day-to-day level, in the world of the book of Revelation, but once we have started to see it, we cannot continue in this world as if nothing had happened either. We are like the 'wise men' of T. S. Eliot's poem, 'Journey of the Magi', who have seen the Christ child and now can never go back to the way things were, as they returned to their former kingdoms 'no longer at ease' in the 'old dispensation': the familiar made new, alien even, by our grasping of the strange new world within the Bible.

To see the world with unveiled eyes, as it is portrayed in Revelation, *should* leave us 'no longer at ease here'. And it should draw us constantly back to the Bible to keep our vision of God, and of God's way of seeing reality, fresh and powerful in our own lives.

Concluding Hermeneutical Postscript: The Word of Life and the Pursuit of Wisdom

♦

This book has been based on the idea that our goal in reading the Bible is to read it wisely: to have eyes to see. Like Eliot's wise men, that can be a disconcerting experience, but it is one which allows Scripture to come alive for us and capture something of the ferocious creative energy of the Word of God which lurks within it. That the Bible remains to so many a boring and frustrating book is one of the great sadnesses of the modern Church, where making sure that we think the right thing has often been more important than opening our eyes to see just what is going on in Scripture.

It seems only fair to conclude this journey with a brief attempt to say what I actually think wisdom is, and look at one place where Scripture encourages us to pursue it. My way of thinking about wisdom is to say that it is the ability to see the world as God would have us see it. So it involves revelation, and it involves being given eyes to see, and it involves developing wise habits of reading Scripture which will allow us to discern 'God's breath' in it: its inspiration and the ways in which we can 'apply' it to ourselves. To do all or any of these also involves investing in the technical abilities to read the biblical text in historical and literary context, with all the challenges and rewards which this revealed in our earlier chapters. Above all, it is to read the Bible always on the road to Emmaus, always in a hermeneutical circle (or spiral) of interaction between Christ and the Scriptures. By way of a conclusion which holds all these ideas together, and draws us towards our overall goal of *Reading the Bible Wisely*, let us turn briefly to the letter of James.

James tends to get a bad press among theologians. It is always known as the book which says 'faith without works is dead' (James 2.17), and that is far from being fully representative of its teaching. In many ways it is the book in the New Testament which is most concerned with wisdom.

At its beginning, James offers the following advice: 'If any of you is lacking in wisdom, ask God, who gives to all generously and ungrudgingly, and it will be given you' (1.5). This seems simple enough, and who would not then ask for it and . . . become wise? There must be a catch. In fact the catch is stated immediately, so it hardly counts as small print. Here it is: 'But ask in faith, never doubting' (1.6) since the one who doubts is nothing less than 'double-minded', and 'unstable in every way'. That seems a bit harsh, and it can in practice lead to the awful experience of trying ever harder to pray for something by screwing up enough faith to *really* believe that it will happen, a defeating and downward-spiralling experience if ever there was one. Surely there must be some other way to understand this passage?

I think the answer lies in understanding what wisdom is. There is a lot of technical background information which is relevant here, to do with the concept of wisdom in the Old Testament, and the personification of wisdom which we find in Proverbs 8.22–31, which many scholars say becomes fully personified in Jesus himself in the New Testament. I could believe that, and the resultant idea that once again the answer is Jesus, in terms of saying that our quest to be wise is our quest to be 'like Jesus', although this needs a lot of careful handling to work out exactly in what ways we are meant to be like Jesus. But clearly in broad outline this is an argument which looks promising. My interest here, however, is simpler, and consists of saying that wisdom is seeing things how God wants us to see them (and perhaps in that sense Jesus represents the perfect way of seeing the world as God's creation, the way God wants us to live in it).

If this is what wisdom is here, then there is a reason why we must believe that God can answer our prayer when we pray for wisdom, because a God who can make us wise is one aspect of the world we must see in order to be wise, and if we doubt that God can do it then we are imagining a world which is not the world God wants us to see. Thus, in a sense, this particular prayer request is a self-fulfilling one, if we pray it the right way (or, in James's words, God will give generously to all who ask it), and if we pray it the wrong way, it cannot possibly work. This does not solve all the problems of those prayers in the New Testament where sufficient faith is the requirement, and it does not mean that doubt does not have a proper place in certain situations, but for this particular prayer, for wisdom from God, it explains the qualifications that James puts on it.[1]

This very ability to see the world this way is there right at the start of James, in the startling verse which exhorts us, 'whenever you face trials of any kind [to] consider it nothing but joy' (1.2). The ability to see a trial as a joy is not a characteristic of the trial we are going through, but of ourselves and whether or not we have eyes to see.

James is rightly known as a practical letter, and it appeals often for that reason. In 1.21 we read 'Rid yourselves of all sordidness and rank growth of wickedness, and welcome with meekness the implanted word that has the power to save your souls'. I have yet to meet anyone who has read this who does not want to do what it says. But how? How can we rid ourselves of all that is wicked within us? Is this our work? Again, the answer is 'Yes and No'. We are to receive, says James, the implanted word within us. What word is that? As we look back over the preceding passage, we come across a pair of verses which go right to the heart of our whole topic of reading the Bible wisely. Wisdom, life, cleanness from sin, these are all gifts of the God who is the giver of every good and perfect gift (1.17). This is the God who gave us birth by the word of truth (1.18). To receive salvation, or life, or to rid ourselves of what is rotten within us, is to hold on to the word of truth.

This word of truth, I think, is the same word which is elsewhere called the word of life, or which is characterized as the Word of God in various places in Scripture. To be wise, then, is to know that any insight we have is from God, and that any time we see with wise eyes these eyes were the gift of God. It is the reminder that by ourselves we are unable to attain wisdom, despite the frequent reduction of the gospel in our Christian lives to standards of morality, to the application of principles, to the constant doomed attempt to 'try harder' one more time, and really please God this time. When we give up this attempt to show God that we are basically all right, then he accepts us as the mess of 'sordidness and wickedness' that we are, and reminds us that he has given us birth by his word of truth.

Wisdom is not a cheap option, and according to Proverbs 4.7 it will cost all we have. 'Whatever else you get, get it,' says Proverbs. The wisdom to be Christ-like. The wisdom to see the world as God wants us to see it. The wisdom to read the Bible as God would have us read it, with open eyes, or better: with eyes opened, just like the disciples on the road to Emmaus.

Notes, References and Further Reading

♦

For each chapter, notes from the text along with full references are given first, and are followed by details of any general works which have contributed to the overall picture built up in that chapter.

1 Reading the Bible as Christian Scripture

Notes

1 J. B. Green, *The Gospel of Luke* (NICNT; Grand Rapids, Eerdmans, 1997), p. 842. His section on the Emmaus story is pp. 840–51.
2 Green, *Luke*, p. 844.

Further reading

Other helpful treatments of the Emmaus story from a hermeneutical point of view include:

S. Hauerwas, *Unleashing the Scripture* (Nashville, Abingdon Press, 1993), pp. 47–62, a sermon on Luke 24 entitled 'The Insufficiency of Scripture: Why Discipleship is Required'.

R. W. L. Moberly, *The Bible, Theology, and Faith* (Cambridge, Cambridge University Press, 2000), pp. 45–70, on 'Christ as the Key to Scripture: The Journey to Emmaus'.

N. T. Wright, *The Challenge of Jesus* (London, SPCK, 2000), pp. 114–33, entitled 'Walking to Emmaus in a Postmodern World'.

2 Reading the Bible as a Historical Book

Notes

1 Tractate *Avot* ('Fathers') 1.1.

2 From the *Talmud b. Ber.* 28b.
3 A. C. Thiselton, *The Two Horizons: New Testament Hermeneutics and Philosophical Description* (Carlisle, Paternoster, 1980), p. 14.

Further reading

J. Neusner (tr.), *The Mishnah: A New Translation* (New Haven, Yale University Press, 1988). This is the version of the *Mishnah* quoted in this chapter.
G. Theissen, *The Shadow of the Galilean* (London, SCM Press, 1987). A novel which draws on a lot of background material to depict the world in which the gospel stories take place.

3 Reading the Bible as a Literary Work

Notes

1 M. Kähler, *The So-Called Historical Jesus and the Historic, Biblical Christ* (Philadelphia, Fortress Press, 1964 (orig. 1896)), p. 80.
2 As argued also by D. Gooding, *According to Luke* (Leicester, IVP, 1987), p. 9.

4 The Difficulty and Clarity of Scripture

Notes

1 L. T. Johnson, *The Writings of the New Testament: An Interpretation* (rev. edn; London, SCM Press, 1999), p. 344.
2 K. Stendahl, *Paul Among Jews and Gentiles* (Philadelphia, Fortress Press, 1976), pp. 78–96.
3 K. Stendahl, *Final Account: Paul's Letter to the Romans* (Minneapolis, Fortress Press, 1995), p. 10.

Further reading

R. H. Bainton, *Here I Stand: A Life of Martin Luther* (Nashville, Abingdon Press, 1978 (orig. 1950)). A good source for the information on Luther.

My reading of Romans has been informed and challenged by the excellent commentaries of J. D. G. Dunn, *Romans* (Word Biblical

Commentary 38A and 38B; Waco: Word, 1988), and C. E. B. Cranfield, *The Epistle to the Romans* (ICC; 2 vols; Edinburgh, T&T Clark, 1975, 1979), as well as the work of Stendahl, above, and N. T. Wright, *The Climax of the Covenant* (Edinburgh, T&T Clark, 1991).

5 The Inspiration and Canon of Scripture

Notes

1 See S. Motyer, *Antisemitism and the New Testament* (Cambridge, Grove Books, 2002), for a good discussion of this difficult issue.
2 My recommendation would be D. C. Allison, *The Sermon on the Mount* (New York, Crossroad, 1999).
3 A very useful survey can be found in D. G. Bloesch, *Holy Scripture: Revelation, Inspiration & Interpretation* (Downers Grove, IVP, 1994), pp. 85–130.
4 R. W. Funk and R. W. Hoover (eds), *The Five Gospels* (New York, Macmillan, 1993).
5 Quoted in Bloesch, *Holy Scripture*, p. 85.

6 The Authority and Application of Scripture

Notes

1 D. J. A. Clines, *What Does Eve Do to Help?* (Sheffield, JSOT Press, 1990), p. 48.
2 W. Brueggemann, *The Bible and Postmodern Imagination* (London, SCM Press, 1993), pp. 61–2.
3 K. Barth, 'The Strange New World Within the Bible', in his *The Word of God and the Word of Man* (London, Hodder & Stoughton, 1928), pp. 28–50.
4 Barth, 'Strange New World', p. 38.
5 N. T. Wright, 'How can the Bible be Authoritative?', *Vox Evangelica* 21 (1991), pp. 7–32.
6 C. F. D. Moule, *Forgiveness and Reconciliation* (London, SPCK, 1998), p. 223.

7 Unveiled Eyes and Unveiled Text

Notes

1 I follow here the argument of R. Bauckham, *The Climax of Prophecy* (Edinburgh, T&T Clark, 1993), pp. 243–57. This work and Bauckham's shorter book, *The Theology of the Book of Revelation* (Cambridge, Cambridge University Press, 1993), have profoundly influenced my approach to the book of Revelation.

Concluding Hermeneutical Postscript

Notes

1 A form of this argument goes back to Kierkegaard. I found it in T. H. Polk, *The Biblical Kierkegaard: Reading by the Rule of Faith* (Macon, Mercer University Press, 1997), pp. 121–5.